KIMBERLY
einmo

modern
QUILTS &
more

American Quilter's Society
P.O. Box 3290 • Paducah, KY 42002-3290
Fax 270-898-1173 • e-mail: orders@AQSquilt.com

Located in Paducah, Kentucky, the American Quilter's Society (AQS) is dedicated to promoting the accomplishments of today's quilters. Through its publications and events, AQS strives to honor today's quiltmakers and their work and to inspire future creativity and innovation in quiltmaking.

EXECUTIVE BOOK EDITOR: ELAINE BRELSFORD
SENIOR EDITOR: LINDA BAXTER LASCO
COPY EDITOR: CHRYSTAL ABHALTER
GRAPHIC DESIGN: ELAINE WILSON
COVER DESIGN: MICHAEL BUCKINGHAM
QUILT PHOTOGRAPHY: CHARLES R. LYNCH
HOW-TO PHOTOGRAPHY: KIMBERLY EINMO
AUTHOR'S PHOTO: KEN EINMO

Additional copies of this book may be ordered from the American Quilter's Society, PO Box 3290, Paducah, KY 42002-3290, or online at www.AmericanQuilter.com.

Text © 2014, Author, Kimberly Einmo
Artwork © 2014, American Quilter's Society

Library of Congress Cataloging-in-Publication Data

Einmo, Kimberly.
  Modern quilts & more / by Kimberly Einmo.
    pages cm
  ISBN 978-1-60460-134-3
  1. Quilting--Patterns. I. Title.
  TT835.E448 2014
  746.46--dc23
                        2014011566

COVER: ORANGE ZEST, detail. Full quilt on page 32.

TITLE PAGE: DRESDEN DAISIES, detail. Full quilt on page 67.

OPPOSITE: ZIG ZAG STARS, detail. Full quilt on page 41.

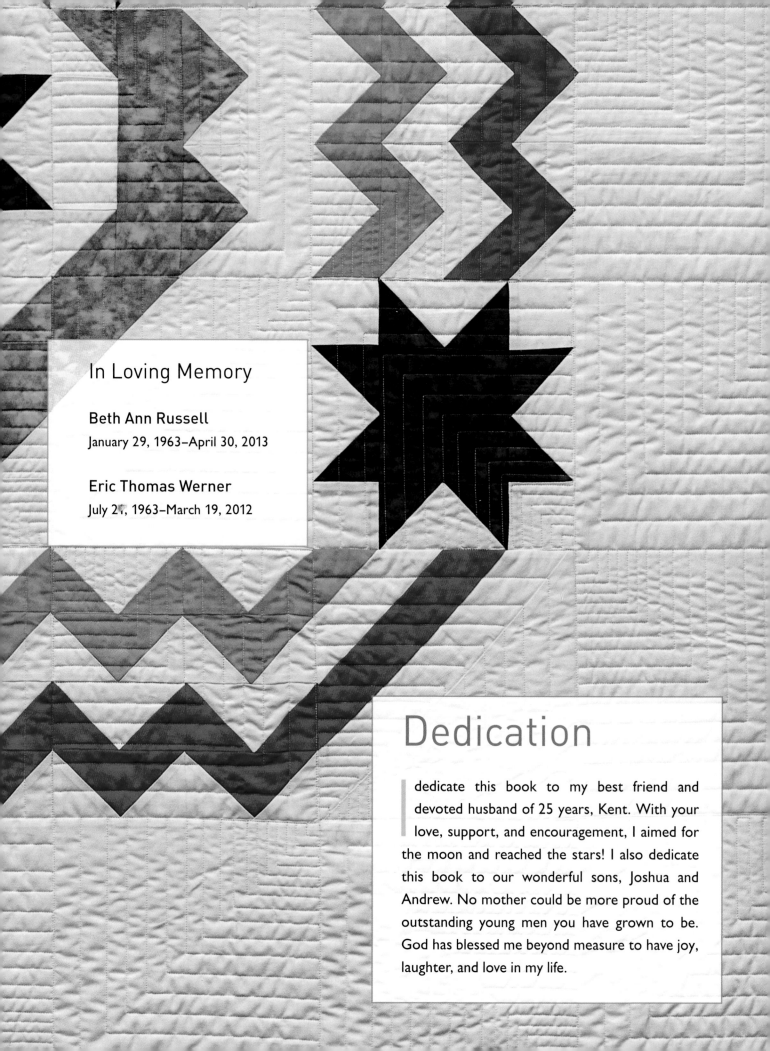

In Loving Memory

Beth Ann Russell
January 29, 1963–April 30, 2013

Eric Thomas Werner
July 2?, 1963–March 19, 2012

Dedication

I dedicate this book to my best friend and devoted husband of 25 years, Kent. With your love, support, and encouragement, I aimed for the moon and reached the stars! I also dedicate this book to our wonderful sons, Joshua and Andrew. No mother could be more proud of the outstanding young men you have grown to be. God has blessed me beyond measure to have joy, laughter, and love in my life.

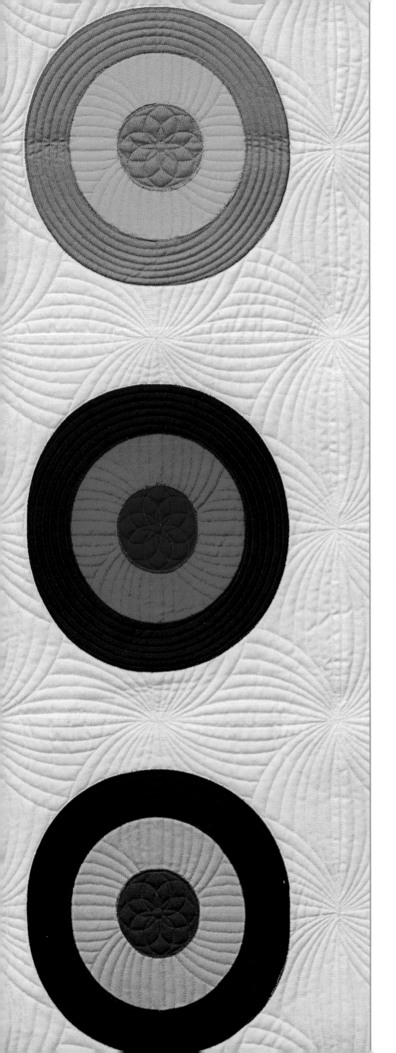

Contents

OPPOSITE: COLOR WHEELS, detail. Full quilt on page 22.

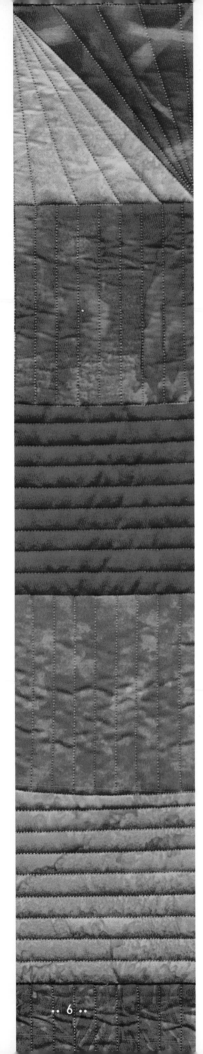

Acknowledgments

There are many people who helped to make this book possible and words seem so inadequate to fully express my heartfelt gratitude for their time, support, and all the ways in which they shared their talents. I want to thank my sweet family. Without their support, encouragement, and patience, this book simply would not have become a reality.

The following talented women have played an integral part behind the scenes of many of the quilts in this and my previous books. These gals road-tested patterns, shared ideas, and sewed like crazy to help me get the job done and meet deadlines. I'd like to recognize and sincerely thank:

Birgit Schüller (Creative BiTS) for sharing her gifted and exquisite quilting talents, her time and creative ideas, and for lending a listening ear throughout our many fun Skype sessions!

Claire Neal for being a dear friend and one of the most talented piecers I know! She has road-tested more of my designs than anyone, and I appreciate her precise sewing and eye for catching errors more than words can say.

Carolyn Archer (Ohio Star Quilting) for her keen eye and ability to visualize how to make my quilt tops sing with her gorgeous longarm quilting, attention to detail, and willingness to try new things outside her comfort zone.

Judi Madsen (Green Fairy Quilts) for adding her completely innovative artistry to my quilt tops to capture the modern aesthetic brilliantly. I'm delighted to call her my friend, and will watch as her star continues to rise with her extraordinary talent and unique quilting abilities!

LEFT: ORANGE ZEST, detail. Full quilt on page 32.

Christine LaCroix (Quilt Patch Deco Quilting) for her talent and willingness to do whatever it takes to get the job done with a cheerful attitude and attention to detail. I'm delighted she is always up for a challenge!

Stevii Graves for stepping in and helping me just when I needed it most! She expertly and beautifully pieced several tops when deadlines were looming. I so love working with her!

Shelly Pagliai (Prairie Moon Quilts) for being so willing to step up and take me on as a new client when she has so many already! She came highly recommended from a mutual friend (thanks, Pat Sloan!) and I am looking forward to working more with her in the future.

Miriam Fay (Carolyn Archer's mom) for sewing so many sleeves and finishing so many bindings!

I'd like to wholeheartedly thank my publisher, Meredith Schroeder; my editors Elaine Brelsford, Andi Reynolds, and Linda Lasco; graphic designer Elaine Wilson; and all the many creative and talented people at the American Quilter's Society. I am so grateful for my long-standing association with them since 2004.

A huge thank you to the following folks for their very generous support for supplying the beautiful fabrics, threads, batting, sewing machine, and furniture used to make the quilts in this book:

Hayden Lees, Timeless Treasures
Kyle Sanchez, Robert Kaufman Fabrics
Bruce and Diane Madigan, SewBatik Fabrics
Lissa Alexander, Moda Fabrics/United Notions
Alex Veronelli, Aurifil Threads
Penny McMorris, Electric Quilt Company
Jeanne Cooke, BERNINA USA
Ed Moore and Susanne Voss, Koala Cabinets
Tricia Santamaria and Judy Novella
    Fairfield Processing Corporation

Introduction:
Modern Quilts at a Glance

honestly think this introduction was the most difficult part of the book for me to write. Why? Because as far as modern quilting goes, how can anyone truly define let alone capture the concept in words? Research on the Internet always ended in my spending countless hours online reading various definitions from a vast number of sources, each claiming to be the true definition of what modern quilting really is all about. While I think there are some similarities and good points made by each of these sources, I don't think there is any one, all-encompassing, objective definition of modern quilts today.

I believe several factors have influenced the growth of the modern quilt movement since the 1990s including a shift in design aesthetics, affordability of digital cameras, and the rise of social media such as blogs, quilt-alongs, and Facebook.

After spending another unproductive morning at the computer, I asked myself what would I rather be doing—searching for the definition of a modern quilt or actually making one? The answer was a no-brainer! So I won't spend time or space here quoting other peoples' definitions. To me it certainly isn't that important but of course you are welcome to do your own Internet search on the subject. I think you'll be amazed by the vast number of ideas and responses you'll get. But ultimately, why waste the time when you could actually be sewing?

Although I have been teaching quilting for more than twenty years (has it really been that long?), I have seen a gradual shift to a more modern design aesthetic not only in my own quilts but also

LEFT AND OPPOSITE: ORANGE ZEST, detail. Full quilt on page 32.

in my students' quilts. During the past ten years or so, many of the modern quilts that have been featured in quilt shows, books, periodicals, and blogs have been constructed using improvisational piecing. While this can be liberating for some people, I find that many quilters, myself included, are happier and more at ease using traditional construction methods.

I'm not talking about using antiquated methods such as cardboard templates and scissors. By traditional methods, I mean rotary cutting, precision piecing, and fast and efficient techniques to make the best use of your quilting time. In fact, I'm quite sure that many traditionally based quilters are attracted to the clean, crisp, bright, and bold "modern look." But in some cases I think they have felt left out or even intimidated by the modern movement if they didn't embrace those improvisational, whack-and-sew-with-abandon methods.

Until now.

I believe it is possible to create beautiful, dynamic, modern quilts using traditional blocks and construction methods. That's exactly what this book is all about! I've taken basic, simple, recognizable, traditional units and blocks and set them together using fast and easy construction techniques. There's nothing improvisational here! The overall designs are modern, crisp, and clean, and the fabrics used to create the quilts in this book are easy to find and replicate. In many cases, I simply shopped in my own stash to enhance the fabric line I used or to create the quilt completely. Stash reduction—it's a beautiful thing. What's not to love?

I hope you will be inspired to create your own modern quilts with a traditional twist. So let's not waste another moment. Are you ready to jump right in? Let's do it!

Get Ready—
Before You Begin!

Welcome! I'm absolutely delighted you've chosen to make some (*or all*) of the projects in this book! Before you dive in and get started, I'd like to invite you to *take a little time to read this chapter first!*

I've written this book just as if I'm talking directly to you! I'd like you to consider me as your own personal quilting coach, here to help you every step of the way. I have all sorts of helpful tips to share so keep an eye out for my TOP TIPS along with a few fun surprises. My goal is simply to help you make stunning quilts!

This book is divided into easy-to-use sections designed to make the process manageable for quilters of all skill levels. I invite you to explore my easily accessible website for additional information. You can contact me directly if you wish at www.kimberlyeinmo.com. So, let's begin!

First, a few basic suggestions about modern quilting: Personally, I'm not concerned with who "invented" modern quilting nor do I subscribe to the idea that there are hard and fast rules of what is or isn't considered modern. All the modern quilts featured in this book have their roots in traditional quiltmaking. The blocks or designs are inspired by traditional elements, as are the techniques used to construct them. I admit it, I prefer to use traditional methods for piecing and machine appliqué.

This book is inclusive. It is for traditional quilters and for modern art makers. Simply put, this book is for anyone who wants to make spectacular, modern quilts.

LEFT: ORANGE ZEST, detail. Full quilt on page 32.

Shared Characteristics of Modern Quilts

The definition of modern quilting aside, there are some common characteristics of modern quilts, and these are quite easy to pinpoint. Modern quilts tend to emcompass:

Bright, bold colors and prints
Dynamic elements for maximum impact
Use of solid fabrics
Minimalism
Effective use of negative space
Lack of borders
Asymmetrical designs
Clean lines
High contrast
Dense quilting

Hints for Using Prints

Most of the quilts in this book have been constructed using beautiful batiks, blenders, scrumptious solids, snazzy stripes, and tone-on-tones. These luscious fabrics all lend themselves to the clean, crisp, modern aesthetic. But let me just say this: all of these quilt designs could work just as beautifully with print fabrics. There are thousands of gorgeous print fabrics out there (many of which are waiting patiently in your own stash right now) that would look spectacular in these designs! So don't be afraid of using your favorite printed fabrics. Be creative and try these designs with the printed fabrics you love. Because the blocks of these quilts are traditional in nature, they will work beautifully with prints of all kinds. Really!

A Place for Precuts?

You bet! There's no denying it: those fabulous bundles of strips and squares affectionately known as Jelly Rolls, Layer Cakes, and Charm Squares are a trend that's here to stay. Don't be hesitant about using precut collections to make these quilts. Just add any additional yardage, if required, and have fun!

To Prewash or Not to Prewash

Now that is a question! And the answer, my friend, is truly a matter of personal preference. I used to be a prewashing purist. But then I began working with Jelly Roll® bundles and other precuts and prewashing simply wasn't practical or feasible! However, with some fabrics (particularly batiks) I absolutely think it is prudent to prewash your fabrics. I like to add those dye catchers to the washing machine. They really work!

Stash Busting at Its Best

Most quilters have a fabric stash. Quilters don't hoard fabric; we simply collect it. But the truth is we need to use our fabric collections! There is no better time than now and the quilt designs in this book are perfect for busting your stash or trimming your scrap basket down to size.

Open those boxes and bins and have fun playing in the fabrics you already own. I'll bet you'll find all sorts of fabulous options for using fabrics you've been "saving" for just the right project.

Everything You'll Need:
Fabrics, Tools, and Basic Supplies Simplified!

▼ A place to sew
▼ A chair with good support
▼ Good lighting
▼ Fabric and thread
▼ Long, thin straight pins
▼ Scissors and seam ripper
▼ Marking and basting tools
▼ Rotary cutter, blades, cutting mat, and rulers
▼ Iron with steam capability and clean ironing surface

▼ A sewing machine in good working condition and machine needles handy for frequent replacements

▼ **Specialty sewing feet:** At the very least, you'll need the following accessory feet to construct the quilts in this book:

¼" piecing foot (I use two; one with the guide AND one without the guide.)

Open-toe appliqué foot

Multi-purpose foot

Walking foot

Free-motion foot

▼ **Batting:** You'll find my favorite batting listed in the Resources Guide (page 108).

▼ **Specialty rulers:** I'll be featuring some of my own specialty rulers that I have designed (and a few by other designers) to make many of the quilts in this book. See pages 14 and 108 for details.

▼ **Fusible web:** Generally, I prefer the lite over the heavy-duty weight. The ultimate goal is for quilts constructed with fusible appliqué to drape beautifully!

▼ Temporary tear-away stabilizers

▼ Basic sewing supplies

▼ **A longarm machine quilter:** If you don't plan to quilt your own quilts, take time to find someone you trust to quilt them for you.

▼ Good company

One of the best things you can have in your studio is the company of a furry friend or two. My sweet little dog, Divot, is always with me whenever I'm working at the computer or sewing, and she's often accompanied by our three rescue kitties.

Get Set

Abbreviations

HST	half-square triangle
QST	quarter-square triangle
RST	right sides together
WST	wrong sides together
LOF	length of fabric
WOF	width of fabric
RSU	right-side up
RSD	right-side down

How to Construct the Units

With a ruler, mat, cutter, and some basic rotary-cutting skills, you will be able to make all of the quilts in this book! If you master how to construct a few essential units—the building blocks of quilting—you'll have no trouble assembling any of these quilts.

I have designed a number of rulers and acrylic tools that feature no math, no wasted fabric, and no-stress techniques. These tools truly help quilters make the most of their time and yardage. So I've included these rulers in the instructions and feature diagrams of just how easy they are to use! I've also included a few additional acrylic tools that will give you a more efficient method to construct some of the quilting units. The specialty tools used in this book are:

EZ Flying Geese Ruler by Kimberly Einmo
EZ Jelly Roll Ruler™ by Kimberly Einmo
EZ Dresden Tool by Darlene Zimmerman
EZ Fat Cats Tool by Darlene Zimmerman

LEFT: ORANGE ZEST, detail. Full quilt on page 32.

You can make the blocks in this book using the specialty rulers or you can use more traditional techniques. Choose your method—I provide instructions for both. Let's get started!

Half-Square Triangles (HSTs)

How to Make HSTs Using the EZ Flying Geese Ruler

▼ Place 2 fabric strips RST. *NOTE: If you are right-handed, begin cutting on the left side of the strip unit and cut from left to right. If you are left-handed, begin cutting on the right side of the strip unit and cut from right to left.*

▼ Use Side B (green side) of the ruler to cut the B triangles from fabric strips, rotating the ruler as shown.

▼ Keep the pieces RST and stitch ¼" on the long side of the triangles.

▼ Press the seams closed first, then press the seam allowance toward the darker fabric.

▼ Trim the "dog ears" from the end of the HST unit.

How to Make HSTs Without Using the Specialty Ruler

▼ Place 2 squares RST.

▼ Draw a diagonal line as shown. This is the stitching line.

▼ Cut ¼" from the stitching line and discard the smaller triangles OR sew them together to form a smaller HST unit for another project.

▼ Press the seam toward the darker triangle.

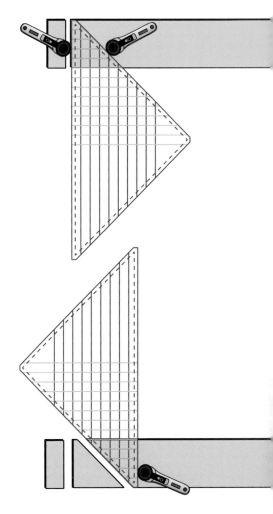

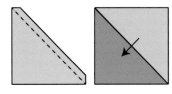

HSTs made using the EZ Flying Geese Ruler

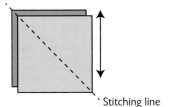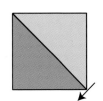

Stitching line

HSTs made without using the specialty ruler

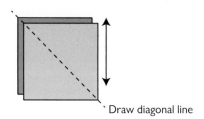

Draw diagonal line

Sew ¼" on both sides of drawn line. Then cut on drawn line.

HSTs made using a traditional method

How to Make HSTs Using a Traditional Method

▼ Place 2 squares RST, ⅞" larger than the desired finished size.

▼ Draw a diagonal line as shown. This will be the cutting line.

▼ Sew ¼" on either side of the drawn line

▼ Cut along the drawn line.

▼ Press the seams toward the darker triangle.

OR

▼ Pair 2 different rectangles as specified in the pattern RST (for example, 2½" x 3¼").

▼ Line up the 45-degree line on your ruler along the bottom of the rectangle unit and draw 2 diagonal lines as shown with a ½" space between the lines. These are the stitching lines .

▼ Stitch on the lines and cut in the middle between the lines (¼" from each stitching line).

▼ Press the seams toward the darker triangles.

▼ Each 3¼" rectangle unit will yield 2 – 2½" x 2½" unfinished HSTs.

▼ Two – 2½" x 40" strips will yield 24 – 2½" x 2½" unfinished HSTs.

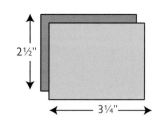

2½"

3¼"

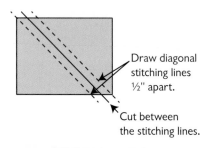

Draw diagonal stitching lines ½" apart.

Cut between the stitching lines.

Flying Geese Units

How to Make Flying Geese Units Using the EZ Flying Geese Ruler

▼ Cut fabric strips according to the FINISHED size of the flying geese units shown on the left side of Side A (magenta side) on the ruler. *NOTE: Two or four layers of fabric strips work best to avoid slippage. Six or more layers result in a loss of cutting accuracy. Trust me on this!*

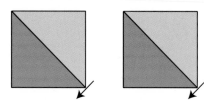

HSTs made using a traditional method

▼ Use Side A to cut center A triangles (QSTs) from the strips. I call these the "geese" units. (See page 21 for an explanation of the difference between QSTs and HSTs.)

▼ Fold the fabric strip RST and use Side B to cut B triangles , or "wings" (HSTs) from strips. This results in mirror-image triangles.

▼ Match notched edge to notched edge and pointed edge to pointed edge. Sew a B triangle (wing) to an A triangle (goose).

▼ Press the unit closed first; then press the unit open with the seam allowance toward the wing.

▼ Sew a B triangle to the other side of the A triangle and press seam allowance toward the second wing.

NOTE: Seam allowances must always be pressed away from the center triangle, even when the wings are a lighter fabric!

▼ Trim the dog ears on the sides.

▼ Square-up the units if necessary.

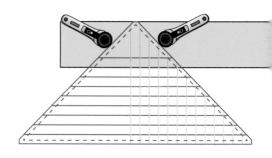
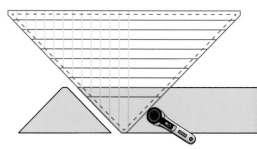

Using side A of EZ Flying Geese Ruler to cut center triangles from strips

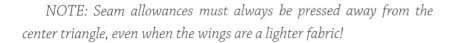

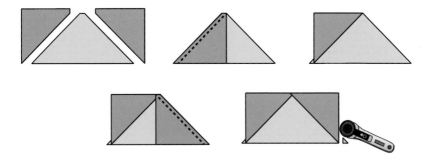

Sew a B triangle to the other side of the A triangle. Trim the dog ears on the sides.

EZ Flying Geese Ruler Handy Strip Reference Chart

You'll definitely want to keep this chart handy (page 18). It will help you calculate the number of triangles you can cut from one strip of fabric (based on a 40" strip). Use this chart to easily convert commercial patterns to cut triangles without wasting any fabric!

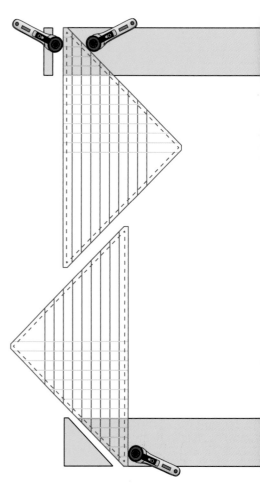

Using side B of EZ Flying Geese Ruler to cut side triangles from strips

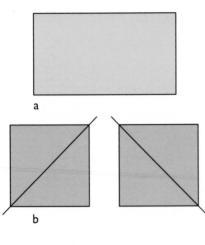

a

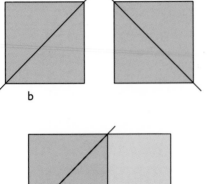

b

Strip Width	# of Triangles from Side A (QSTs)	# of Triangles from Side B (HSTs)
2"	15	26
2½"	13	24
3"	11	22
3½"	9	20
4"	8	18
4½"	7	16
5"	6	13
5½"	5	11
6"	4	9
6½"	5	10

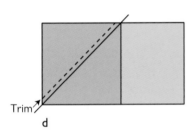

Stitching line

c

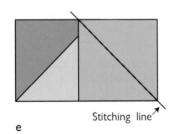

Trim

d

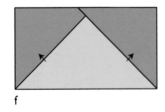

Stitching line

e

How to Make Flying Geese Units Using a Traditional Method

▼ Cut one rectangle (a) the desired unfinished size of the unit (for example, 2½" x 4½") and two contrasting squares the height of the rectangle (in this example, 2½" x 2½").

▼ Draw a diagonal line on the wrong side of both squares (b).

▼ Place a square RST on the rectangle with the diagonal line positioned as shown. Stitch on the line (c).

▼ Trim ¼" from the stitching line (d).

▼ Press the seam away from the rectangle.

▼ Position the other square, stitch on the drawn line, and trim ¼" from the stitching line (e).

▼ Press the seam away from the center triangle (f).

f

How to Use the EZ Jelly Roll Ruler

I designed the EZ Jelly Roll Ruler for using with 2½" strips and precuts but honestly, it has turned out to be my "go-to" ruler for cutting so many different units! Many of the quilts in this book do not require cutting using ⅛" increments, so this ruler is perfect because there are no ⅛" markings. It is clear and easy to use. This versatile 5" x 10" ruler has mint green markings that show up clearly on all fabrics, so you can cut your fabrics into manageable squares, rectangles, or diamonds in a snap! Of course you can use other rulers but I think once you start using this handy-dandy ruler, it will soon become your favorite go-to ruler as well.

How to Cut Squares

▼ Line up the mint green highlight line covering the edge of your strip, matching the width of your strip.

▼ Cut squares as shown.

How to Cut Rectangles

▼ Line up the mint green highlight line along the edge of your strip matching the width of your strip.

▼ Use the ¼", ½", or whole-inch markings to match the length of your desired size. Cut rectangles as shown.

How to Cut Diamonds

▼ Line up the 45-degree line along the bottom (horizontal) edge of your fabric strip. Trim just inside the raw edge to create the first diagonal cut.

▼ Slide the ruler over so the diagonal cut lines up with the width of the fabric strip.

▼ Cut the first diamond as shown.

▼ Continue across the strip for more diamonds, always keeping the 45-degree line along the horizontal edge.

Attention lefties! These instructions work perfectly for you, too. *(My mom, who is left-handed, is my inspiration to always remember left-handed quilters.)* Simply start at the other end of the strip and work from right to left.

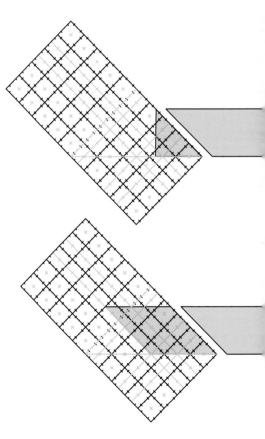

Using the EZ Jelly Roll Ruler to cut squares

Using the EZ Jelly Roll Ruler to cut rectangles

Using the EZ Jelly Roll Ruler to cut diamonds

EZ Jelly Roll Ruler Handy Strip and Square Reference Table

Here are two more charts you'll definitely want to keep within easy reach. They will help you calculate the number of basic units you can cut from strips (based on a 40" strip) and precut squares. Use this chart to easily convert commercial patterns to help you avoid wasting any fabric from your precuts!

Size of Unit	# of Units Cut from a 5" Square	# of Units Cut from a 10" Square
1½" x 1½"	9	36
2½" x 2½"	4	16
2½" x 5"	2	8
5" x 5"	1	4
5" x 10"	0	2

Strip Width	Unit Size	# of Units Cut from a 40" Strip
1½"	1½" x 1½"	26
	1½" x 2"	20
	1½" x 2½"	16
	1½" x 3"	13
	1½" x 3½"	11
	1½" x 4"	10
	1½" x 4½"	8
	1½" x 5"	8
	1½" x 5½"	7
2½"	2½" x 2½"	16
	2½" x 3"	13
	2½" x 3½"	11
	2½" x 4"	10
	2½" x 4½"	8
	2½" x 5"	8
	2½" x 5½"	7

How to Use the EZ Dresden and Fat Cats Tools

▼ Cut fabric strips ½" wider than the finished size of the Dresden wedges or as directed in the pattern.

▼ Align the top of the EZ Dresden or Fat Cats tool on the bottom of the strip as shown and cut on both sides of the tool.

▼ Rotate the tool as shown and continue cutting the desired number of wedges.

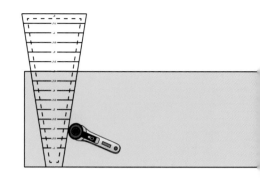

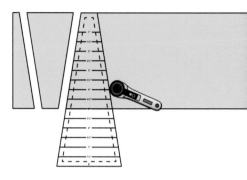

Using the EZ Dresden and Fat Cat tools

HSTs and QSTs—Here's the Difference

Every quilter needs to understand the basic differences between half-square and quarter-square triangles. Consider the square. Assuming it has been cut on the straight-of-grain, as most squares should be, if you cut a square once diagonally, you get two triangles with the straight-of-grain running along the two short sides of the triangle. The bias edge will run along the long side. These triangles are half-square triangles (HSTs) because both halves came from one square.

Consider the same square now cut twice diagonally. You get four triangles with the straight-of-grain running along the long side of the triangle and the bias edges along the two shorter sides. These triangles are quarter-square triangles (QSTs) because four triangles came from one square.

Why is this information about the bias and straight of the grain important to you? Because, every quilter needs to be aware of the placement of these two types of triangles within their blocks. The rule of thumb is this: In most cases the straight-of-grain in every triangle needs to run along the outside edge of the completed unit or block.

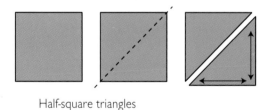

Half-square triangles

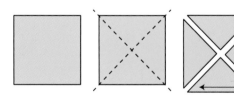

Quarter-square triangles

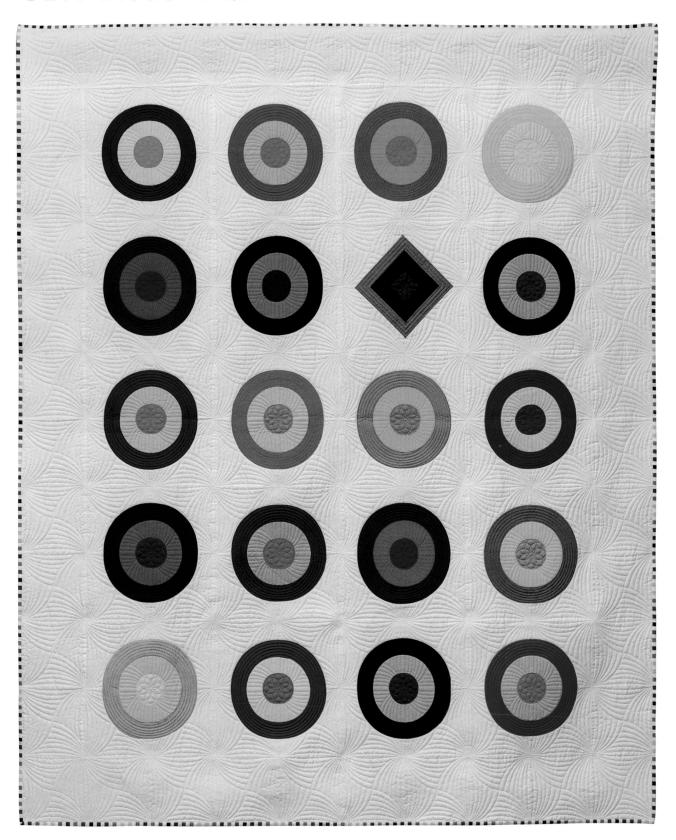

COLOR WHEELS, 60" x 72", designed and made by the author, quilted by Carolyn Archer, Ohio Star Quilting

Color Wheels

This quilt is modern, crisp, and clean. And who can resist a bull's eye of pure, saturated color? These simply fused circles are quick to cut and so easy to machine appliqué! You can use small pieces of fabric or scraps for the circles, but I've made it extra easy for you to gather solid colors together by providing a chart of the Kona cottons I used to make my quilt. The black and gray Diamond block adds a hint of static by standing out from the clear colors. You'll be amazed how quickly this quilt comes together and how much you'll love the creative use of color. It's even more exciting than having a brand new crayon box on the first day of school!

Finished block size:

12" x 12"

Skill level:

Skilled Beginner

Fabric:

Robert Kaufman Kona Cotton Solids

FABRIC	YARDS	INSTRUCTIONS
#1 - Kona Cotton White Background	3¾ yards	*Cut the following pieces from yardage LOF as shown in the cutting layout diagram (page 24).* • Cut 4 – 6½" x 60½" border strips. • Cut 20 – 12½" x 12½" squares.
#2 - Large circles and large diamond	10" x 10" squares of 20 different medium or dark colors including one gray	• Press fusible web to the back of the fabric squares following the manufacturer's instructions. • Cut 19 – 8" circles using the 8" template (page 31). • Cut 1 – 6½" x 6½" square from the gray.
#3 - Medium circles and medium diamond	8" x 8" squares of 20 different light colors including one gray	• Press fusible web to the back of the fabric squares following the manufacturer's instructions. • Cut 19 – 5" circles using the 5" template (page 31). • Cut 1 – 4½" x 4½" square from the gray.
#4 - Small circles and small diamond	5" x 5" squares of 20 different medium or dark colors including one gray	• Press fusible web to the back of the fabric squares following the manufacturer's instructions. • Cut 19 – 2" circles using the 2" template (page 31). • Cut 1 – 2" x 2" square from the gray.

(continued)

(continued)

FABRIC	YARDS	INSTRUCTIONS
Backing	4¾ yards	• 2 panels 34" x 80"
Batting		• 68" x 80"
Binding – Michael Miller #PC5708 Stripe Couture	½ yard	• Cut 7 – 2¼" strips; piece together to make single-fold, straight-grain binding.

Additional supplies:

Open-toe or appliqué presser foot

3 yards lightweight fusible web

3 yards (temporary) tear-away stabilizer

Neutral thread for stitching blocks together

Monofilament or matching 50-wt. cotton thread for machine appliqué

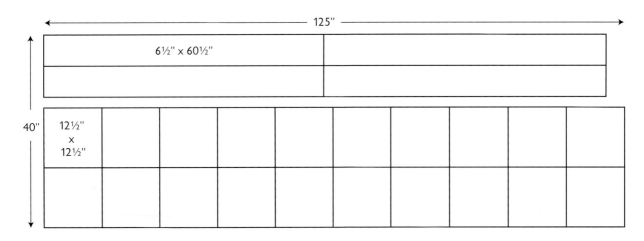

Cutting layout

TOP TIP

Solid fabrics finally have their chance to take a starring role and look absolutely terrific in modern quilts such as this one! Use solids that have been tucked away in your stash, or stock up on solid fat quarters the next time you're at your local quilt shop. Or, on your next birthday or special event you can invest in the *ultimate* collection of luscious solids from Robert Kaufman fabrics! I find it extremely helpful to keep a fabric color card on hand. If you don't have a fabric color card, paint chips work well in a pinch.

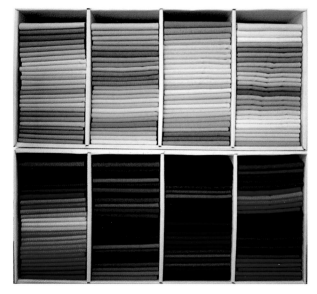

The ultimate solids collection

ABOVE: I gathered together fat quarters of solid fabrics in color groups together before cutting the circles.

ABOVE: I had fun selecting a wide range of colors from Aurifil's 50-wt. cotton threads to match the Kona cotton solid fabrics I used. The spools are simply scrumptious eye candy for quilters!

LEFT: Color chart

These are the Kona Cotton (Robert Kaufman) fabrics I used to make COLOR WHEELS.

Block	#	Color	Block	#	Color
A	144 1234 135	Sour Apple Mint Clover	K	400 1265 323	Carrot Orange Flame
B	1480 1194 1091	Chinese Red Lipstick Crimson	L	1080 1019 359	Coal Black Pepper
C	1061 1005 1135	Candy Green Aqua Emerald	M	1478 149 1479	Yarrow Papaya Amber
D	1214 1383 327	Magenta Violet Tulip	N	1551 1087 1091	Rich Red Coral Crimson
E	1077 1056 1677	Citrus Buttercup Curry	O	142 24 1301	Crocus Petunia Purple
F	1282 1514 139	Peacock Robin Egg Lagoon	P	1089 23 350	Corn Yellow Lemon Cheddar
G	1048 1189 415	Bright Peri Lavender Regal	Q	357 27 1541	Lapis Cornflower Deep Blue
H	1228 1281 419	Melon Peach Azalea	R	1294 143 1066	Plum Petal Cerise
I	405 277 90	Algeria Blueberry Pacific	S	414 199 1703	Peapod Cactus Grass Green
J	1188 21 135	Kiwi Honey Dew Clover	T	141 1062 1295	Carnation Candy Pink Pomegranate

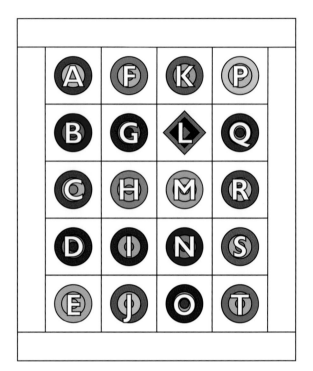

Color placement

Construction

▼ Line up 19 sets of 3 circle shapes and 1 set of 3 gray squares set on point in the center of the background squares and fuse in place using a hot, dry iron. Allow to cool completely.

▼ Cut 20 – 10" x 10" squares of lightweight stabilizer; place one piece of stabilizer beneath each block.

▼ Use a small zigzag or your favorite machine appliqué stitch to sew the shapes to the background.

▼ Bring the thread ends to the wrong side, tie them off, and snip close to the knot for a clean finish on the front of your blocks.

▼ Carefully remove the stabilizer from the back of your blocks.

▼ Arrange the blocks according to the quilt assembly diagram (below). Join the blocks into rows. Sew the rows together.

▼ Press the seam allowances open, especially if using a white or light background fabric.

▼ Add the 6½" background fabric border strips to the quilt top.

▼ Quilt, bind, add a label, and enjoy!

TOP TIP

I auditioned 20 or so different solid fabrics for the binding, but none of them seemed just right. Then I went "shopping" in my stash to look for something different. I found a colorful striped fabric that added the perfect touch of whimsy and an eye-catching "pop" to an already bright, fun, modern quilt. I love it!

Zigzag stitch

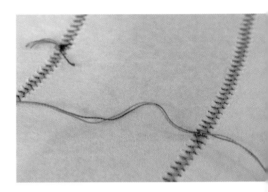

Tie off stitch

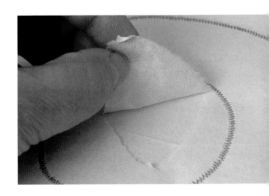

Tear-away stabilizer

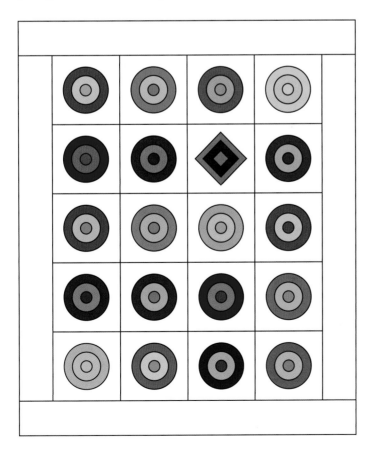

LEFT: Quilt assembly

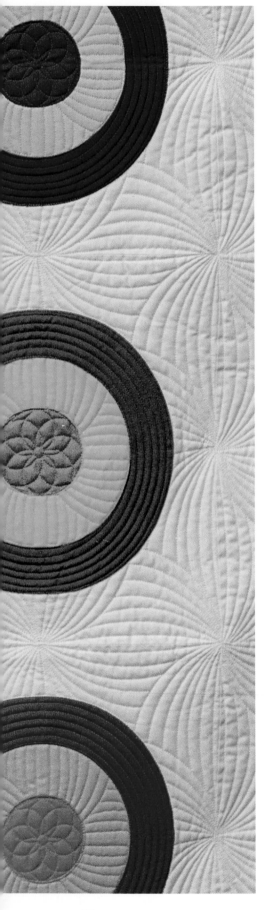

Thoughts about the Quilting from Carolyn

Kimberly sent me a picture of this quilt as a computer graphic before it was pieced so I could get some ideas prior to her sending me the finished top. So many ideas were swimming in my head, it was hard to decide what to do to make this design really sparkle. After going back and forth between design ideas, I ultimately didn't decide until I had the quilt on the frame of my longarm machine. I put three different patterns in the color rings and then a wonderful background pattern from Anita Shackelford called Curved Quad. I took the background pattern all the way out through the borders. Now it appears as if the bull's-eye circles just float on the quilt. Both Kimberly and I are very happy with how this turned out!

Round 2 Re-do: GUMBALLS

Cut more circles to create a fast, fused, and cheerful quilt!

I had so much fun cutting circles from my solid fabrics that I just couldn't stop! I ironed fusible web to the leftover fat quarters of solid fabrics and cut out more circles in large and small sizes. I found a 32" x 40" piece of leftover fabric from another quilt (incidentally, it was Kona Ash solid gray fabric from MODERN CHAIN on page 58) and I scattered the circles across the surface of the fabric. It took less than 30 minutes to decide on an interesting placement and fuse the circles in place.

This time, I didn't machine appliqué the circles to the background. With the dense quilting I had in mind, it wasn't necessary. This was the perfect way to complete this creative, impromptu project! This small quilt or wallhanging is a great way to use up the leftover circles from COLOR WHEELS and is the perfect way to welcome a new baby for a modern-minded mom, or a great addition to the bedroom wall of any 'tween or teenage young lady!

LEFT: COLOR WHEELS, detail. Full quilt on page 22.

A Few Extra Thoughts about the Quilting from Carolyn

I just love quilts you make out of leftovers from a project; they feel like bonus quilts with no added effort or expense. I think they are "sew" creative! This quilt just needed a great texture to give it dimension. I used another modern quilting pattern from Anita Shackelford called Dew Drop. The pattern has simple vertical lines broken up by random circles. It gives the quilt the great texture I envisioned and turns leftovers into a main course. Awesome!

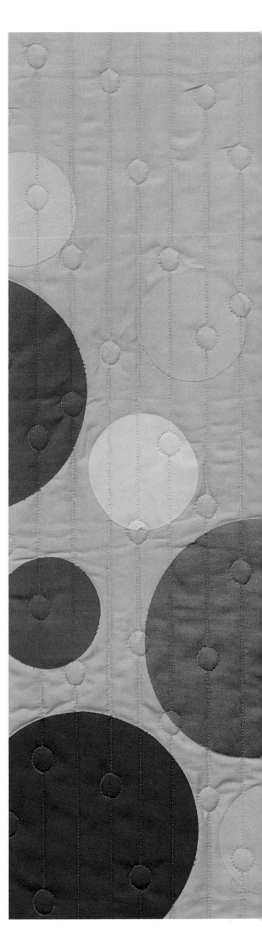

GUMBALLS, 32" x 40", designed and made by the author, quilted by Carolyn Archer, Ohio Star Quilting

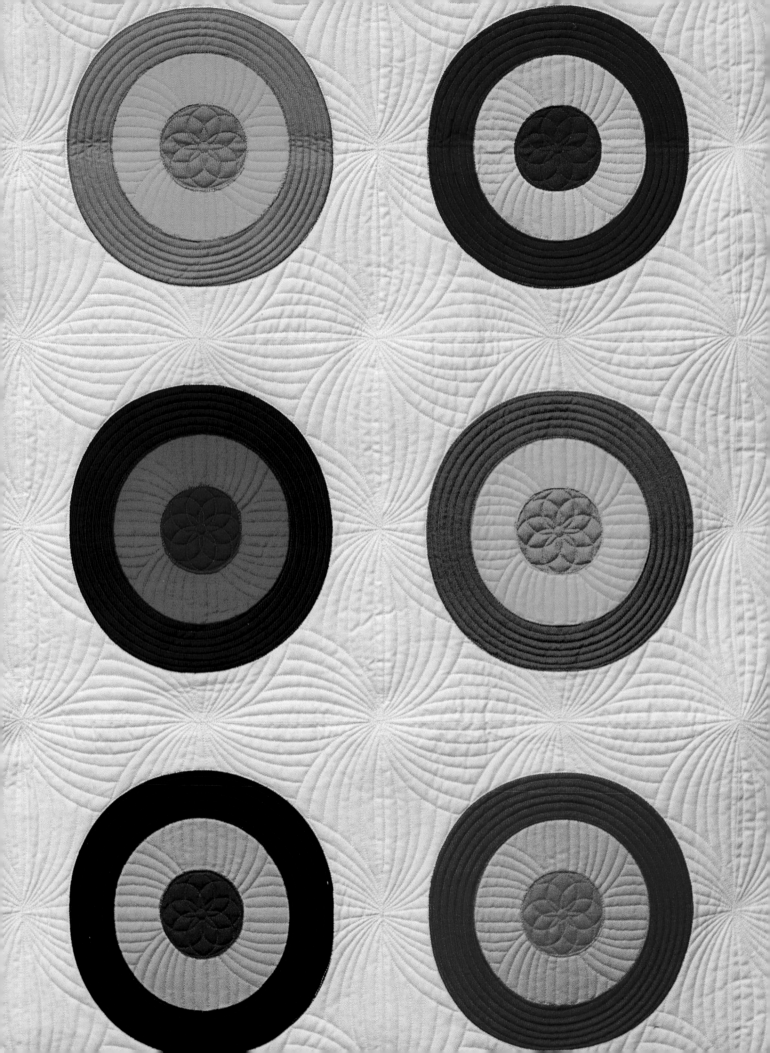

COLOR WHEELS
8"
©Kimberly Einmo

COLOR WHEELS
5"
©Kimberly Einmo

COLOR WHEELS
2"
©Kimberly Einmo

COLOR WHEELS Templates
Full size

ORANGE ZEST, 45" x 54", designed and made by the author, quilted by Judi Madsen, Green Fairy Quilts

ORANGE ZEST

This was the first quilt I created for this book and from the very beginning, I kept referring to it as "the orange quilt" because honestly, coming up with new names for quilts is sometimes the hardest part for me. *(It's true!)* But one day while I was grating an orange peel for a recipe, the idea for the name came to me like a light turning on and I think the name fits perfectly!

The great thing about this quilt is that it's a perfect pattern for a Charm Pack (with at least 31 – 5" x 5" squares) or squares from your stash, plus one background fabric. This quilt will dazzle using almost any color palette of printed, solid, or batik fabrics so pick your favorites and get going. Simple, dramatic, smashing!

Perfect for Charm Packs!
Finished block size:
4½" x 4½"
Skill level:
Skilled Beginner
Fabric:
Kona Cotton and a variety of orange batiks from my stash

FABRIC	YARDS	CUTTING INSTRUCTIONS
#1 – Background *Kona Cotton White*	2⅝ yards	*Cut the following pieces as shown in the cutting layout diagram (page 34)* • Cut 5 – 5" strips; subcut 34 – 5" x 5" squares; and 2 – 5" x 9½" rectangles, • Cut 5 – 9½" strips; subcut 4 – 9½" x 9½" squares; 2 – 9½" x 14" rectangles; 4 – 9½" x 18½" rectangles; and 1 – 9½" x 23" rectangle
#2 – A variety of orange fabrics	¾ total yards	• Select 31 – 5" x 5" squares from a charm pack OR cut 31 – 5" x 5" squares from a variety of fabrics.
Backing	3¾ yards	• 2 panels – 27" x 62"
Batting		• 53" x 62"
Binding	½ yard	• Cut 6 – 2¼" strips; piece together to make single-fold, straight-grain binding.

TOP TIP

I chose a wide variety of orange, yellow, gold, and burnt sienna fabrics (including printed, solids and batiks from my stash) and I cut 5" x 5" squares. It was fun to arrange them in the structured layout of this design because all the shades of orange work so beautifully together! I love this pattern and will probably make it again and again using different color combinations just to see how they'll look together. Experiment and see what modern color combos you can put together or just make yourself a gorgeous ORANGE ZEST quilt like mine!

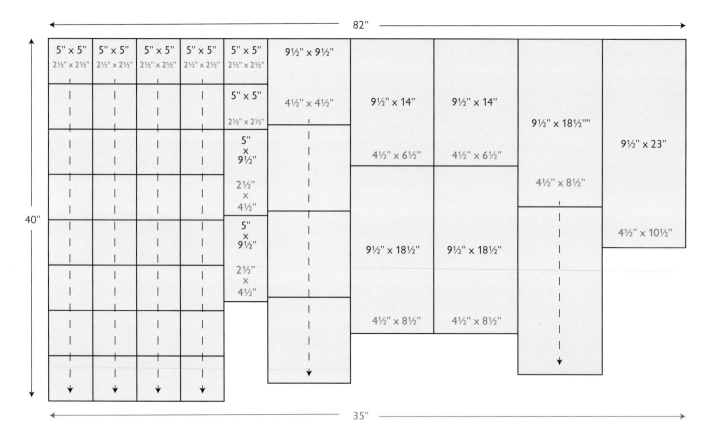

Cutting layout for ORANGE ZEST (black dimensions) and ORANGE ZESTY (green dimensions)

Construction

HST Assembly

▼ Select 10 – 5" x 5" orange squares and set aside.

▼ Select 4 – 5" x 5" orange squares and put them RST in 2 pairs.

▼ Pair the remaining 17 – 5" x 5" orange squares with 17 – 5" x 5" background fabric squares RST.

▼ Draw a diagonal line on the wrong side of each pair of squares.

▼ Sew on the line and trim ¼" from stitching line. Set aside the trimmed fabric triangles for a fun Round 2 Re-do project (page 38).

▼ Press all seams toward the orange triangles.

▼ HSTs should measure 5" x 5" unfinished.

▼ Make 17 – orange/white HSTs and 2 – orange/orange HSTs.

▼ Arrange the blocks according to the quilt assembly diagram (page 36). Join the blocks into rows. Sew the rows together to complete the quilt top.

▼ Quilt, bind, add a label, and enjoy!

HST assembly

Make 17.

Make 2.

TOP TIP

For those of you who love to use the EZ Flying Geese Ruler, this project is the perfect place to use it to make HSTs! You can easily cut Side B triangles from 5" x 5" background strips or your orange strips if you prefer to use yardage and strips rather than charm squares.

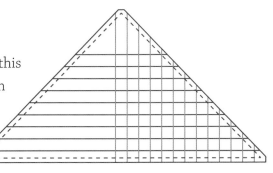

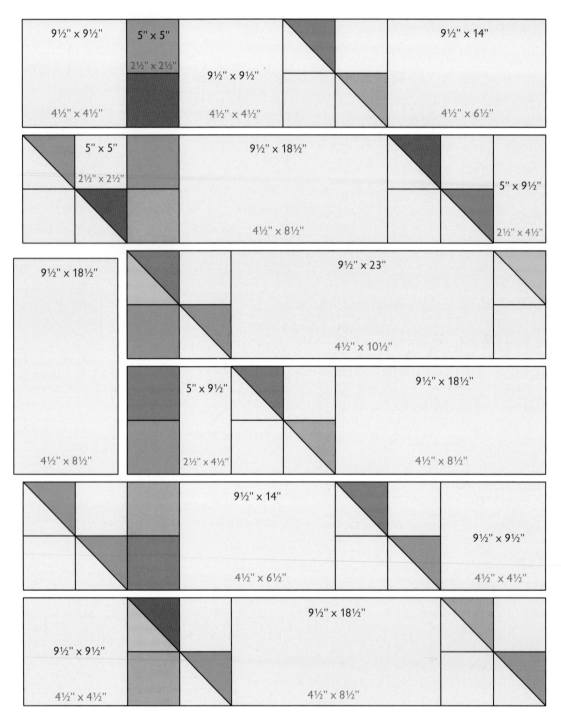

Quilt assembly for ORANGE ZEST (black dimensions) and ORANGE ZESTY (green dimensions)

Thoughts About the Quilting from Judi

Sometimes knowing what to quilt is the hardest part of quilting, but what I love most about free-motion quilting is that you can do any quilting design and make it work nicely for a small or large project. I wanted to create a fun, modern quilting design that did not take a lot of time, so I started with quilting circles and swirls together in a random order. This design would normally be a filler design, but I made it the main design.

To break up the quilting and give this quilt a modern fill, I added in ½" spaced lines. These lines were marked with disappearing ink then stitched using my straight ruler as a guide. The insides of the lines were filled with circles and swirls to pull the quilting all together and provide a consistent look. My last approach for making this quilt more modern was to take on the triangle pieced shapes in the quilt top. Any time you want to add dimension to a quilt, just add in a shape that is pulled from the piecing. I always mark the straight lines, but make sure to keep the shapes random to give the modern feel to the quilting.

RIGHT: ORANGE ZEST, detail. Full quilt on page 32.

ORANGE ZESTY, 20" x 24", designed, made, and quilted by the author

Finished block size:
2" x 2"
Skill level:
Skilled Beginner
Fabric:
Kona Cotton and a variety of orange batiks from my stash

Round 2 Re-do: ORANGE ZESTY

Use the leftover triangles, charm squares, or small pieces from your scraps to create a delightful, mini-version of ORANGE ZEST! Follow the simple cutting instructions and assemble the same way as you would for the larger quilt.

FABRIC	YARDS	INSTRUCTIONS
#1 – Background *Kona Cotton White*	½ yard	*Cut the following pieces as shown in the cutting layout diagram (page 34)* • Cut 34 – 2½" x 2½" squares; 2 – 2½" x 4½" rectangles; 4 – 4½" x 4½" squares; 2 – 4½" x 6½" rectangles; 4 – 4½" x 8½" rectangles; and 1 – 4½" x 10½" rectangle.
#2 – A variety of orange fabrics	¾ total yards	• Cut 10 – 2½" x 2½" squares cut from a variety of fabrics. • Cut 17 – 2½" x 2½" squares cut from a variety of fabrics to make HSTs. **OR** see directions page 39 to use up leftover triangles trimmed from 5" HSTs.
Backing	¾ yard	• 24" x 28"
Batting		• 24" x 28"
Binding	¼ yard	Cut 3 – 2¼" strips; piece together to make single-fold, straight-of-grain binding.

ORANGE ZESTY Assembly

▼ Use charm squares, scraps, and leftover triangles trimmed from the 5" HSTs construction.

▼ Select 10 – 2½" x 2½" orange squares and set aside.

▼ Cut 4 – 2½" x 2½" orange squares and put them RST in 2 pairs to make 2 orange/orange HSTs.

▼ Pair 17 – 2½" x 2½" orange squares with 17 – 2½" x 2½" background fabric squares RST and make 17 orange/white HSTs (page 35) to measure 2½" x 2½" unfinished.

▼ Assemble the mini quilt by following the quilt assembly diagram (page 36).

Try This!

As promised, here's an easy technique to use the leftover triangles trimmed from the 5" HSTs.

▼ Sew a ¼" seam on the long side of the trimmed triangle units.

▼ Press the seam toward the dark fabric. HST should measure 4¼" unfinished.

▼ Use a ruler (the EZ Jelly Roll Ruler works perfectly) and trim a 2½" x 2½" square from the triangle unit.

▼ Make 17 – 2½" white/orange HSTs and 2 – 2½" orange/orange HSTs.

Thoughts About the Quilting from.....Me!

I quilted this little version of ORANGE ZEST on my Baby Lock® Sashiko machine and had so much fun! This specialty machine uses thread only in the bobbin—there's no top thread at all—and makes stitches that look like hand quilting.

Using leftover triangles trimmed from the 5" HSTs

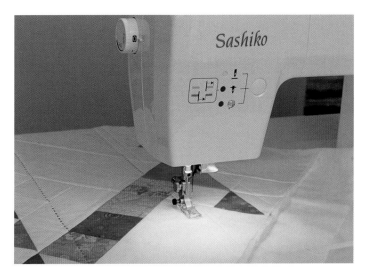

Machine quilting with a hand-quilted look

It was especially exciting to use a heavier weight, (Aurifil 28-wt.) variegated cotton thread so the stitches take center stage and add an extra, snazzy element to the design. I also used 40-wt. white thread to add additional texture without overpowering the quilt design with "too much of a good thing."

Of course, you can easily machine quilt ORANGE ZESTY on your home sewing machine or practice your hand quilting stitches. It's a project small enough to see immediate results. Whatever you choose to do, I encourage you to step out of your quilting comfort zone and try something new for you. Treat yourself to a spool of gorgeous, variegated orange thread, try free-motion quilting, or test drive the Sashiko machine at your local Baby Lock dealer! The small size of ORANGE ZESTY makes it a great project to continue to build your skills and, of course, have fun in the process!

TOP TIP

I recommend using Fairfield's Fusi-Boo® Fusible Blended Fiber Batting for small quilted projects like ORANGE ZESTY, especially if you plan to use the Sashiko or other sewing machine for big-stitch style quilting stitches. The batt fuses beautifully to both the quilt top and backing fabric and prevents any shifting or puckering as you stitch.

LEFT: ORANGE ZESTY, detail. Full quilt on page 38.

ZIG ZAG STARS, 56" x 56", designed by the author, made by Claire Neal, Newport News, Virginia, and quilted by Carolyn Archer, Ohio Star Quilting

Zig Zag Stars

Finished block size:

8" x 8"

Skill level:

Skilled Intermediate

Fabric:

Fresco Fabrics by Patrick Lose for Robert Kaufman

This modern design packs a visual punch with just four concentrated colors and a white background fabric, and the modern quilting takes a starring role without overpowering the pieced elements. If you love making flying geese units and Sawtooth Stars, you'll really enjoy making this modern version of traditional quilt elements. While it isn't difficult to piece, take your time to match points and seams to make the blocks flow together effortlessly. This design has movement, texture, and a bit of static that makes it absolutely eye-catching in so many ways.

Additional Supplies

EZ Flying Geese Ruler (optional)

Instructions for the traditional method are listed in RED. Instructions for using the EZ Flying Geese Ruler are listed in BLUE. Everything listed in BLACK applies to both methods. Cut all strips from WOF except as indicated for the background fabric.

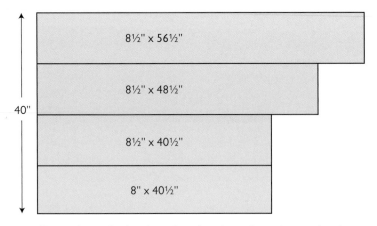

Cutting layout for borders. Cut after the quilt top is completed.

FABRIC	YARDS	CUTTING INSTRUCTIONS
#1 – Background Creamy white APL 11834-87 Snow	4 yards	• Cut 1 – 8⅞" strip; subcut 2 – 8⅞" x 8⅞" squares. Cut squares once diagonally to yield 4 triangles (you will only use 3). • Cut 1 – 8½" strip; subcut 3 – 8½" x 8½" squares. • Cut 2 – 2" strips; subcut 3 – 2" x 12½" rectangles and 3 – 2" x 7" rectangles. • Cut 3 – 2½" strips; subcut 4 – 2½" x 8½" rectangles and 4 – 2½" x 4½" rectangles. Set aside the third strip until you cut the #4 fabrics. • Cut 2 – 2½" strips; subcut 20 – 2½" x 2½" squares. • Cut 1 – 2½" strip to make HSTs. • Subcut 4 – 2½" x 3¼" rectangles. • Cut 8 Side B triangles. **To make flying geese units:** • Cut 15 – 2½" strips; subcut 64 – 2½" x 4½" rectangles and 128 – 2½" x 2½" squares. • Cut 11 – 2½" strips; cut 64 Side A triangles. Then fold 5 strips RST and cut 64 pairs of Side B triangles. Set aside the remaining fabric to cut the borders after the quilt top is completed. • 1 – 8½" x 56½" strip (bottom border) • 1 – 8½" x 48½" strip (top border + 1 Star block) • 2 – 8½" x 40½" strips (side borders)
#2 – Orange APL – 11834-149 Apricot	⅝ yard	• Cut 1 – 2⅞" strip; subcut 2 – 2⅞" x 2⅞" squares. Cut squares once diagonally to yield 4 triangles (you will only use 3). **For the flying geese units, cut:** • 6 – 2½" strips; subcut 22 – 2½" x 4½" rectangles and 44 – 2½" x 2½" squares. • 4 – 2½" strips; cut 22 Side A triangles. Then fold 2 strips RST and cut 22 pairs of Side B triangles.
#3 – Red APL – 11834-116 Tomato	½ yard	• Cut 1 – 2" strip; subcut 3 – 2" x 9¾" rectangles. **For the flying geese units, cut:** • 6 – 2½" strips; subcut 22 – 2½" x 4½" rectangles and 44 – 2½" x 2½" squares. • 4 – 2½" strips; cut 22 Side A triangles. Then fold 2 strips RST and cut 22 pairs of Side B triangles.
#4 – Green APL – 11834-38 Chartreuse	½ yard	• Cut 1 – 4⅜" strip; subcut 3 – 4⅜" x 4⅜" squares. • Cut 1 – 2½" strip; pair with #1 – 2½" strip and set aside. • Cut 1 – 2½" strip to make HSTs: • Cut 4 – 2½" x 3¼" rectangles. • Fold strip RST and cut 8 pairs of Side B triangles. **For the flying geese units cut:** • 1 – 2½" strip; subcut 8 – 2½" x 4½" rectangles. • 1 – 2½" strip; cut 8 Side A triangles. • Cut 1 – 2½" strip; subcut 4 – 2½" x 8½" rectangles.

(continued)

(continued)

FABRIC	YARDS	CUTTING INSTRUCTIONS
#5 – Purple APL – 11834-251 Heliotrope	⅓ yard	• Cut 1 – 4½" strip; subcut 5 – 4½" x 4½" squares. **For the flying geese units, cut:** • 3 – 2½" strips; subcut 40 – 2½" x 2½" squares. • 2 – 2½" strips; fold in half RST and cut 20 pairs of Side B triangles.
Backing	3¾ yards	• 2 panels 32" x 64"
Batting		• 64" x 64"
Binding	½ yard	• Cut 7 – 2¼" strips; piece together to make single fold, straight grain binding.

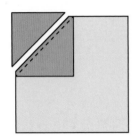

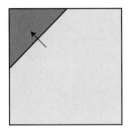

Block 1 – Make 3

Block 1

For each block you will need:

▲　1 – 4⅜" x 4⅜" square from fabric #4

▲　1 – 8½" x 8½" square from fabric #1

▼　Draw a diagonal line on the back of the 4⅜" x 4⅜" square.

▼　Place the marked square RST on the corner of a fabric #1 – 8½" x 8½" square as shown.

▼　Sew on the drawn line; trim ¼" from seam line to remove excess fabric.

▼　Press fabric #4 out to create a square.

▼　Make 3 blocks.

▼　The blocks should measure 8½" x 8½" unfinished.

HST Assembly

Traditional method (page 16)

▼　To make HSTs, place 4 – fabric #1 and fabric #4 – 2½" x 3¼" rectangles RST.

▼　Stitch on drawn diagonal lines and trim in the middle of the sewn lines.

▼　Press the seam allowances toward the darker fabric.

▼　Make 8 – 2½" x 2½" HSTs.

EZ Flying Geese method (page 15)

▼　To make HSTs, place 2½" Side B fabric #1 and fabric #4 triangles RST.

▼　Stitch ¼" from raw edge of triangles and press the seam toward the darker fabric.

▼　Make 8 – 2½" x 2½" HSTs.

Flying Geese Assembly

▼ Follow directions on page 18 to make flying geese units using the traditional method.

▼ Follow directions on page 17 to make flying geese units using the EZ Flying Geese Ruler.

▼ ALWAYS press seams toward side triangles, and don't forget to trim all dog ears.

▼ Flying geese units should measure 2½" x 4½" unfinished.

TOP TIP

From this step forward, I don't recommend squaring-up any of your blocks until you construct all the blocks for the quilt. Be consistent with your scant ¼" seam as you sew your blocks. When you have finished constructing the blocks, measure each of them and then square them all to a consistent size. Trust me, you'll be glad you waited until just before assembling the entire quilt top to true-up your blocks. While the blocks are not technically difficult, these units can be a little bit pesky to piece. But I am confident you are up to the challenge!

Block 2

For each block you will need:
- ▲ 1 – 2½" x 8½" rectangle from fabric #1
- ▲ 2 – flying geese units from fabrics #1 sides/#4 centers
- ▲ 1 – 2½" x 8½" rectangle from fabric #4
- ▲ 2 – 2½" x 2½" HSTs from fabrics #1/#4
- ▲ 1 – 2½" x 4½" fabric #1 rectangle

▼ Make 4 blocks.

▼ Press the seams as shown.

▼ The blocks should measure 8½" x 8½" unfinished.

Make 20 – #5 side triangles and #1 center triangles.

Make 8 – #1 side triangles & #4 center triangles.

Make 22 – #3 side triangles & #1 center triangles.

Make 22 – #1 side triangles & #3 center triangles.

Make 22 – #2 side triangles & #1 center triangles.

Make 22 – #1 side triangles & #2 center triangles.

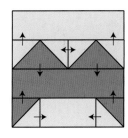

Block 2 – Make 4.

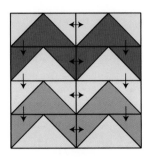

Block 3 – Make 11.

Block 3

For each block you will need:

- ▲ 2 – flying geese units from fabrics #1 sides/#3 centers
- ▲ 2 – flying geese units from fabrics #3 sides/#1 centers
- ▲ 2 – flying geese units from fabrics #1 sides/#2 centers
- ▲ 2 – flying geese units from fabrics #2 sides/#1 centers

▼ Make 11 blocks.

▼ Press the seams as shown, being careful to press center seam open.

▼ The blocks should measure 8½" x 8½" unfinished.

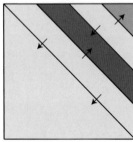
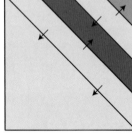

Block 4 – Make 3

Block 4

For each block you will need:

- ▲ #1 – 2" x 7" rectangle
- ▲ #3 – 2" x 9¾" rectangle
- ▲ #1 – 2" x 12½" rectangle
- ▲ #2 – 2⅞" triangle
- ▲ #1 – 8⅞" triangle

▼ Trim each end of the rectangles using the 45-degree line on your ruler to create 3 trapezoids.

▼ Join the trapezoids and the smaller #2 triangle as shown.

▼ Add a fabric #1 – 8⅞" triangle to complete the block.

▼ Make 3.

▼ Press the seams as shown.

▼ The blocks should measure 8½" x 8½" unfinished.

Trim each rectangle

Block 5

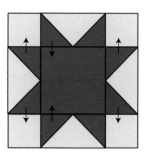

Block 5 – Make 5.

For each block you will need:

- ▲ 4 – 2½" fabric #1 squares
- ▲ 4 – flying geese units from fabrics #5 sides/#1 centers
- ▲ 1 – 4½" fabric #5 square

▼ Make 5 blocks.

▼ Press the seams toward the squares as shown.

▼ The blocks should measure 8½" x 8½" unfinished

▼ Arrange the blocks according to the quilt assembly diagram (below). Join the blocks into rows. Sew the rows together to complete the quilt top.

▼ Cut and add border strips from fabric #1 background fabric, with one star block in the upper left corner.

▼ Quilt, bind, add a label, and enjoy!

Quilt assembly

Thoughts About the Quilting from Carolyn

I had to study this quilt top for a few days before I figured out what quilting design would work best. When planning to quilt a modern quilt, you have to look at the quilt differently than when you are planning traditional quilting. With traditional quilting you need to look at the piecing and try to accentuate it. But with modern quilting you want to create movement and texture and often times, the pieced design may not be entirely relevant and you can disregard it altogether.

After contemplating this quilt top for some time, I decided to use a geometric square pattern called Modern Logs by Anita Shackelford. I saw that the whole quilt was constructed of the same sized squares. Some squares were pieced and some weren't. I used the squares and not the piecing as placement guides for the quilting pattern and therefore was able to create an allover texture that complemented the piecing but wasn't guided by it. The end result is exactly what this quilt needed to really sparkle!

Try This!

When I was teaching at AQS Quilt Week in Lancaster, Pennsylvania, I had just a few minutes after teaching class to see the vendors before the show closed, so I asked my editor if she had seen anything that was new, different, or really "hot." Linda quickly whipped out a long, thin, fabric-

LEFT: ZIG ZAG STARS, detail. Full quilt on page 41.

covered stick from her bag and said, "THIS will change your quilting life." I laughed at the idea but agreed to find the vendor's booth where she had bought The Strip Stick. I bought one, and later at home I tested this so-called must-have quilting notion. OH-MY-GOODNESS . . . she was right! This seemingly not-so-glamorous invention DID change my life! Here's why.

There are times when you are piecing blocks that it is actually better to press the seams open rather than to one side. But pressing ¼" seam allowances open is tricky at best and many times ends in pain with burned fingertips. But with this wonderful invention, you simply lay your block on top of the stick, run your iron along the seam, and it magically falls open with no fuss and no burned fingers! More often now, especially with diagonal seams or where many seams come together at an intersection, I find myself pressing my seams open rather than to one side and my blocks lie flatter and seams with many points are easier to match. I keep one on my ironing board at all times. I don't know how I ever lived without The Strip Stick! (See the Resource Guide, page 109.)

RAINBOW CONNECTION, 77" x 77", designed and made by the author, quilted by Birgit Schüller, Creative BiTS

Rainbow Connection

Years ago, I bought 14 fat quarters of hand-dyed fabrics while I was at a quilt show. They were so beautiful that for a long time I simply couldn't bear to cut them. But I realized I would enjoy them ever-so-much more pieced into a beautiful quilt to admire and appreciate rather than hiding, unused, in a dark cupboard in my stash. I waited for the perfect opportunity to use them and designed this modern quilt specifically to showcase their beauty.

Diamonds, while traditional in nature, really sparkle in contemporary designs and since these blocks are easily pieced with no set-in or "Y" seams, anyone can make this gorgeous quilt. But if you don't fancy a rainbow palette, this modern quilt would look just as smashing with big, bold print fabrics in any number of dynamic color combinations.

Fat Quarter Fabulous!
Finished block size:
  9½" x 9½"
Skill level:
  Skilled Intermediate
Fabric:
  Kona Cotton by Robert Kaufman and hand-dyed fabrics

FABRIC	YARDS	CUTTING INSTRUCTIONS
#1 – Background Kona Cotton White (includes binding)	4⅞ yards	*First, cut pieces WOF from 40" x 66" as shown in cutting layout diagram a (page 52).* • 3 – 6⅝" strips; subcut 18 – 6⅝" x 6⅝" squares. • 3 – 5" strips; subcut 24 – 5" x 5" squares. • 1 – 6⅝" strip; subcut 2 additional 6⅝" x 6⅝" squares. Trim the remaining strip to 5" and cut 3 – 5" x 5" squares. • 9 – 2¼" x 40" strips; piece together to make single-fold, straight-of-grain binding. *Cut pieces from remaining yardage 40" x 97" LOF as shown in cutting layout diagram b (page 52).* • 2 – 6⅝" strips; subcut 22 – 6⅝" x 6⅝" squares. • 1 – 5" strip; subcut 15 – 5" x 5" squares. • 7 – 10" x 10" squares. *I recommend waiting until your quilt top is pieced to cut the borders.* • 2 – 5½" x 77" strips for the side borders. • 2 – 5½" x 67" strips for the top and bottom borders.

(continued)

(continued)

FABRIC	YARDS	CUTTING INSTRUCTIONS
#2 – Diamonds Selection of rainbow fabrics	14 fat quarters (18" x 22") OR ⅜ yard from each of 14 fabrics	*For the diamonds cut 3 strips from each fat quarter as shown in cutting layout diagram c (below).* • Cut 6 diamonds (2 from each strip) from each of 14 fabrics (84 total). • **OR,** if using 40" wide fabric, cut 2 – 4½" strips from each of 14 fabrics; subcut 6 diamonds from each (84 total).
Backing	5 yards	• 2 panels 43" x 85"
Batting		• 85" x 85"

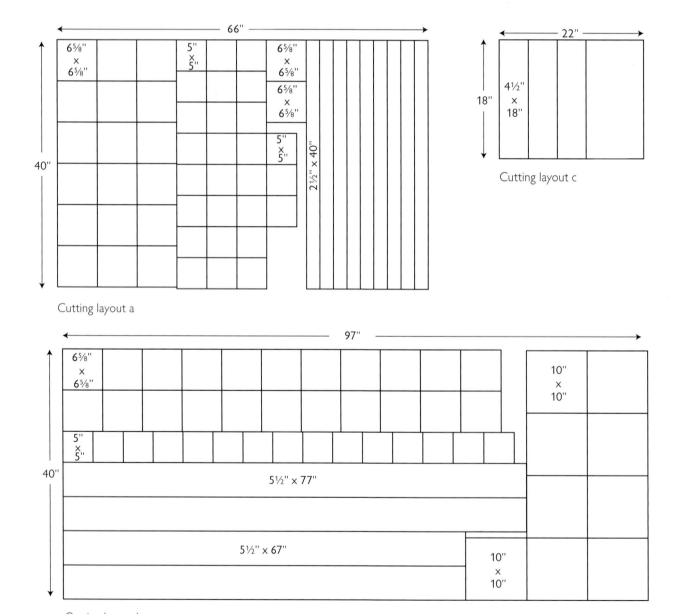

Cutting layout a

Cutting layout c

Cutting layout b

TOP TIP

You'll make best use of your fat quarter by cutting 4½" strips and using your ruler to cut the diamonds. You'll have an 8½" x 18" strip left over.

Attention lefties! These instructions work perfectly for you, too. *(My mom, who is left-handed, is my inspiration to always remember left-handed quilters.)* Simply start at the other end of the strip and work from right to left.

Construction

▼ Cut all 42 – 5" x 5" fabric #1 squares once diagonally to yield 84 – A triangles.

▼ Cut all 42 – 6⅝" x 6⅝" fabric #1 squares once diagonally to yield 84 – B triangles.

▼ Lay out a single block as shown.

▼ Place an A triangle RST on a diamond and line up the points and two raw edges as shown.

▼ Stitch along the long side of triangle A; repeat for the other diamond. (These are mirror-image units.)

NOTE: The A and B triangles are cut a tiny bit oversized, so follow your scant ¼" seam carefully!

▼ Sew a B triangle to the first diamond and another B triangle to the opposite side of the other diamond.

▼ Always press the seams toward the background fabric triangles and not toward the diamonds *(even when using white fabric!).*

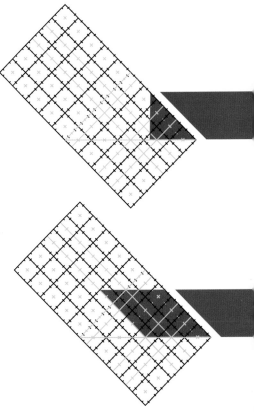

Using the EZ Jelly Roll Ruler to cut diamonds

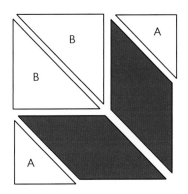

Block 1

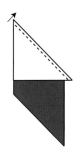

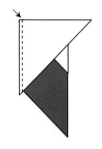

B triangle sewn to diamond

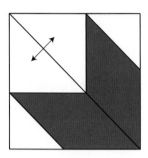

Diamond wedge units sewn together
and center seam pressed open

Little trimmings

▼ Trim any excess background fabric before sewing the diamond wedge units together.

▼ Sew the diamond wedge units together and press the center seam open.

▼ Blocks should measure 10" x 10" unfinished.

▼ Make 3 blocks in each of 14 colors (total 42).

Top Tip

To make your blocks lie flat, you absolutely need to square-up your blocks before sewing them into the quilt. Even with the most accurate cutting and ¼" seams, there will always be the small bits that need to be trimmed or your blocks will be more difficult to sew together and your quilt certainly won't lie flat. So don't skip this all important step! You can see just how many little trimmings I had left over after squaring-up all 42 of my blocks!

▼ Arrange the blocks according to the quilt assembly diagram. Join the blocks into rows. Sew the rows together.

▼ Add 5½" border strips of #1 background fabric to complete the quilt top.

▼ Quilt, bind, add a label, and enjoy!

Quilt assembly

Thoughts about the Quilting from Birgit

Diamonds cut from wonderful jewel-tone, hand-dyed fabrics arranged in an awesome rainbow-style gradation were the inspiration for doing extensive ruler work on the quilt surface. I created a somewhat orderly crisscross of straight and curved lines. I used DeLoa Jones' Boomerang rulers in three sizes to quilt the continuous-line network in the background using white thread and the line system that fans out from a central point in between two pieced Diamond blocks each using matching thread colors.

After this line quilting was done, an obvious unquilted path was left between the two design sections of the quilt. Here I chose to take up the diamond piecing theme and I quilted a string of different size diamonds through the diagonal. I echo quilted these diamonds once and then logically extended the background

RIGHT: RAINBOW CONNECTION, detail. Full quilt on page 50.

DIAMOND STAR COLOR WHEEL 1, 19" x 19",
made by the author

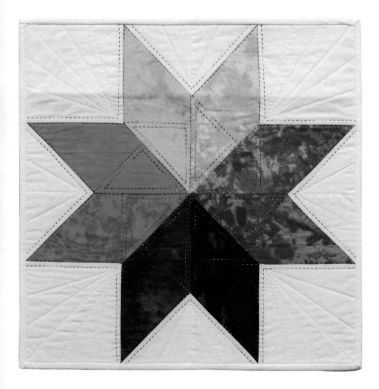

DIAMOND STAR COLOR WHEEL 2, 19" x 19",
made by the author

crisscross of quilted curved lines to connect the individual sections of the quilt to a homogeneous entity.

Since this top has a border of background fabric where the pieced design has not been extended to the very edges, I decided to boycott this border impression by extending the quilting of the diamond section to the edges. I did this using the same thread colors as in the immediately neighboring diamond sections.

Round 2 Re-do: DIAMOND STAR COLOR WHEEL

I had plenty of leftover fabric from each of my hand-dyed fat quarters, so I thought it would be fun to make two fast and easy little quilts. Choose a fun new background fabric from your stash (you'll need about ⅓ yard). For a different twist on these diamonds, simply use one diamond cut from each of 8 fabrics (4 blocks) to make a fast and colorful DIAMOND STAR quilt—perfect to hang on your sewing studio wall!

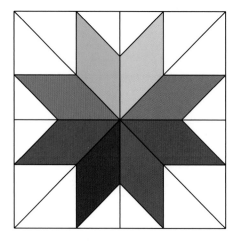

Color Wheel block

A Few Extra Thoughts about the Quilting from...Me!

I enjoy experimenting with different quilting motifs and designs on quilt tops that are exactly the same to see how the quilting "makes the quilt." I had the opportunity to do just that because I made two of these cute little DIAMOND STAR COLOR WHEEL quilts. I used my Sashiko machine and 28-wt. rainbow variegated cotton thread on both to create big-stitch quilting stitches. I marked the quilting lines with a Hera marker and ruler.

For the first quilt I quilted long lines through the middle extending to the star points and also at marked intervals in each diamond. In the white background fabric, I used 40-wt. white cotton thread to quilt evenly spaced lines echoing the angles created by the star.

For the second quilt I used my EZ Flying Geese Ruler to mark symmetrical geese units rotating in a clockwise direction around the center of the star to create a lovely pinwheel effect. I stitched on these marked lines and also ¼" away from the lines to create an echo effect in the geese. Instead of quilting in the ditch, I quilted right next to the ditch (the seam lines) so the stitches would show and not get lost in the actual seam. In the background I used 40-wt. white cotton thread and quilted straight lines that radiate outward from the angle points.

Both quilting options are very effective and I like them both so much, I can't decide which is my favorite!

DIAMOND STAR COLOR WHEEL 1 and 2, details. Full quilts on page 56.

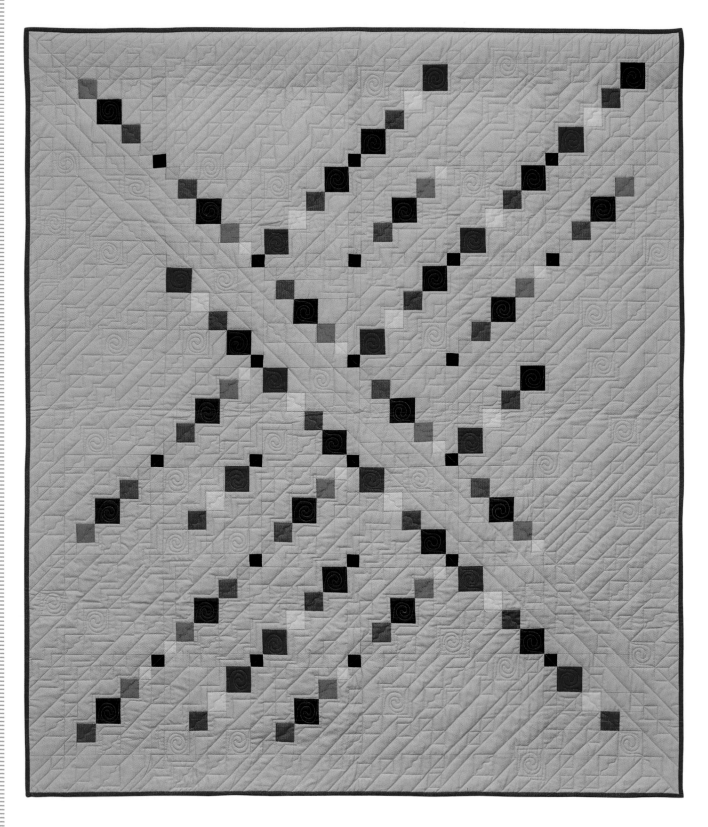

MODERN CHAIN a.k.a. THE CIRCUIT BOARD QUILT, 54" x 62", designed by the author,
made by Claire Neal, Newport News, Virginia, quilted by Shelly Pagnali, Prairie Moon Quilts

MODERN CHAIN a.k.a. THE CIRCUIT BOARD QUILT

Chain blocks have such traditional links to the past, but there's no reason they can't be modernized! And here's the perfect proof: I've updated a version of an Irish Chain block and combined it with a classically cool, cranberry, and gray color scheme with a fresh new layout for a quilt that speaks volumes about today's modern style. You will only cut squares and rectangles for this quilt, which makes construction especially easy!

Fabrics listed are from Robert Kaufman Kona Cotton Solids. This quilt isn't at all difficult to piece but you will definitely want to make a fabric "legend" to keep all those similar shades of color organized for careful fabric placement within the blocks. Simply make a copy and glue small fabric bits in the chart shown below. Cut strips LOF and WOF as indicated the cutting layout diagram.

> **⅛ Yard Cuts Are Perfect!**
> **Finished block size:**
> 7" × 7"
> **Skill level:**
> Skilled Beginner
> **Fabric:**
> Robert Kaufman Kona
> Cotton Solids

TOP TIP

Keep a sticky notepad handy and label all your pieces as you cut them.

PATCH	SIZE	PATCH	SIZE
A	1½" × 6½"	G	2½" × 2½"
B	2" × 5"	H	1½" × 7½"
C	2½" × 3"	I	2½" × 5½"
D	1½" × 2"	J	2" × 4"
E	1½" × 1½"	K	2" × 2½"
F	2" × 2"	L	2½" × 7½"

FABRIC	YARDS	CUTTING INSTRUCTIONS	FABRIC LEGEND
#1 – Ash (Gray, for background)	3¼ yards	Cut the following pieces from the yardage LOF according to the cutting layout diagram. The B# labels indicate placement in the quilt top. • 1 – 8½" x 31½" rectangle (B1) • 1 – 8½" x 23½" rectangle (B2) • 1 – 8½" x 8½" square (B4) • 2 – 8½" x 15½" rectangles (B3) • 1 – 8½" x 7½" rectangle (B5) • 1 – 1½" x 15½" rectangle (B6) • 51 – 1½" x 7½" rectangles (3 H patches and 48 for sashing) • 2 – 3½" x 56½" strips (outer border) • 2 – 3½" x 53½" strips (outer border) Cut the remaining pieces WOF according to the cutting layout diagram. • 1 – 6½" strip; subcut 27 – 1½" x 6½" A patches. • 2 – 5" strips; subcut 30 – 2" x 5" B patches. Trim the remainder of the strip to 2 – 2" strips and cut a total of 30 – 1½" x 2" D patches. • Cut 2 – 3" strips; subcut 30 – 2½" x 3" C patches. • 1 – 7½" strip; subcut 3 – L patches. Trim the remaining strip to 5½"; cut 1 more 5½" strip and cut a total of 25 – 2½" x 5½" I patches. • Cut 2 – 4" strips; subcut 28 – 2" x 4" J patches. Trim the remaining strip to 2½"; cut 1 more 2½" strip and cut a total of 28 – 2" x 2½" K patches. • 3 – 1 ½" x 7" H patches for Block 2.	
#2 – Carnation	⅛ yard	• Cut 1 – 1½" strip; subcut 15 1½" x 1½" E patches.	
#3 – Pomegranate	⅛ yard	• Cut 1 – 2" strip; subcut 15 – 2" x 2" F patches.	
#4 – Dark Violet	⅛ yard	• Cut 1 – 2½" strip; subcut 15 – 2½" x 2½" G patches.	
#5 – Bright Pink	⅛ yard	• Cut 1 – 2" strip; subcut 15 – 2" x 2" F patches.	
#6 – Petal	¼ yard	• Cut 1 – 1½" strip; subcut 12 – 1½" x 1½" E patches. • Cut 1 – 2" strip; subcut 14 – 2" x 2" F patches.	
#7 – Cerise	⅛ yard	• Cut 1 – 2½" strip; subcut 14 – 2½" x 2½" G patches.	
#8 – Berry	⅛ yard	• Cut 1 – 2½" strip; subcut 11 – 2½" x 2½" G patches.	
#9 – Plum	⅛ yard	• Cut 1 – 2" strip; subcut 14 – 2" x 2" F patches.	
#10 – Hibiscus	⅛ yard	• Cut 1 – 1½" strip; subcut 21 – 1½" x 1½" E patches.	

(continued)

(continued)

FABRIC	YARDS	CUTTING INSTRUCTIONS	FABRIC LEGEND
Backing	4 yards	• 2 panels 31" x 70"	
Batting		• 62" x 70"	
Binding	⅝ yard	• Cut 8 – 2¼" strips; piece together to make single-fold, straight-of-grain binding.	

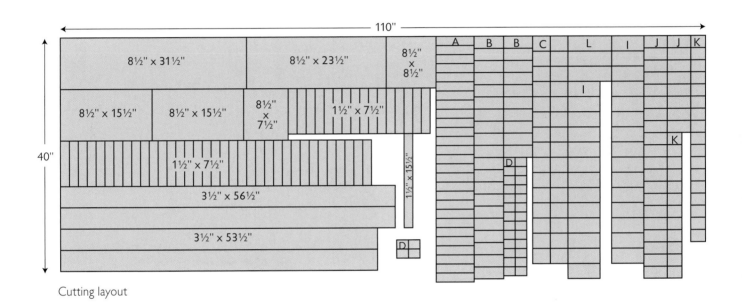

Cutting layout

TOP TIP

I can almost hear the groans as you look at the background fabric cutting chart above. I realize the amount of cutting for this quilt looks daunting. But trust me, you'll be done before you know it, especially if you tackle cutting all of the background fabric first. And the most important thing you can do to make the task feel effortless is to change your rotary blade! A new, sharp blade in your rotary cutter will make your cutting seem like a hot knife going through butter!

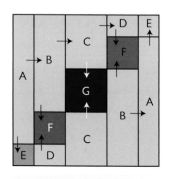

Block 1 – Make 12.

Construct 12 Block 1

▼ For each block you will need:
   ▲ 1 – 1½" x 1½"   fabric #2 E patch
   ▲ 1 – 2" x 2"   fabric #3 F patch
   ▲ 1 – 2½" x 2½"   fabric #4 G patch
   ▲ 1 – 2" x 2"   fabric #5 F patch
   ▲ 1 – 1½" x 1½"   fabric #6 E patch

▼ For each block from fabric #1 (background), you will need:
   ▲ 2 – 1½" x 6½"   A patches
   ▲ 2 – 2" x 5"   B patches
   ▲ 2 – 2½" x 3"   C patches
   ▲ 2 – 1½" x 2"   D patches

▼ Make 12 blocks; press all seams as shown by the arrows.

▼ The blocks should measure 7½" x 7½" unfinished.

Construct 3 Block 2

▼ For each block you will need:
   ▲ 1 – 1½" x 1½"   fabric #2 E patch
   ▲ 1 – 2" x 2"   fabric #3 F patch
   ▲ 1 – 2½" x 2½"   fabric #4 G patch
   ▲ 1 – 2" x 2"   fabric #5 F patch

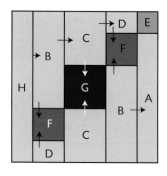

Block 2 – Make 3.

▼ For each block from fabric #1 (background) you will need:
   ▲ 1 – 1½" x 6½"   A patch
   ▲ 2 – 2" x 5"   B patches
   ▲ 2 – 2½" x 3"   C patches
   ▲ 2 – 1½" x 2"   D patches
   ▲ 1 – 1½" x 7½"   H patch

▼ Make 3 blocks; press all seams as shown by the arrows.

▼ The blocks should measure 7½" x 7½" unfinished.

Construct 11 Block 3

▼ For each block you will need:
  ▲ 1 – 2½" x 2½" fabric #7 G patch
  ▲ 1 – 2" x 2" fabric #6 F patch
  ▲ 1 – 2" x 2" fabric #9 F patch
  ▲ 1 – 2½" x 2½" fabric #8 G patch

▼ For each block from fabric #1 (background) you will need:
  ▲ 2 – 2½" x ½" I patches
  ▲ 2 – 2" x 4" J patches
  ▲ 2 – 2" x 2½" K patches

▼ Make 11 blocks; press all seams as shown by the arrows.

▼ The blocks should measure 7½" x 7½" unfinished.

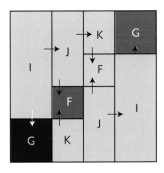

Block 3 – Make 11.

Construct 3 Block 4

▼ For each block you will need:
  ▲ 1 – 2½" x 2½" fabric #7 G patch
  ▲ 1 – 2" x 2" fabric #6 F patch
  ▲ 1 – 2" x 2" fabric #9 F patch

▼ For each block from fabric #1 (background) you will need:
  ▲ 1 – 2½" x 5½" I patch
  ▲ 2 – 2" x 4" J patches
  ▲ 2 – 2" x 2½" K patches
  ▲ 1 – 2½" x 7½" L patch

▼ Make 3 blocks; press all seams as shown by the arrows.

▼ The blocks should measure 7½" x 7½" unfinished.

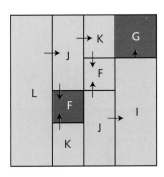

Block 4 – Make 3.

▼ Arrange the blocks, sashing strips, cornerstones, and background pieces in rows within the center section and in columns along the sides according to the quilt assembly diagram (page 64).

▼ Join the blocks and sashing strips into rows. Join the sashing strips and cornerstones into rows.

▼ Join the rows.

▼   Sew the sections together.

▼   Add 3½" border strips from fabric #1 background fabric to complete the quilt top.

▼   Quilt, bind, add a label, and enjoy!

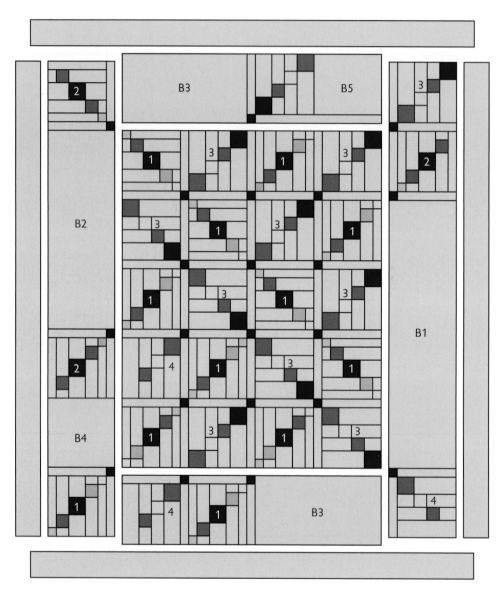

Quilt assembly

Thoughts about the Quilting from Shelly

When Kimberly asked me to quilt one of her quilts for her newest book, I was so excited, but nervous, too! We were both going to be at AQS QuiltWeek® 2013 in Paducah, so we agreed to meet there to exchange the quilt top and discuss how it should be quilted. Kimberly was teaching classes and I went to see her during the lunch break and there she was sitting with award-winning quilter Susan Stewart! My sister and I had just been on the show floor admiring Sue's top prizewinning quilt, so there I was—in the presence of greatness all around!

Kimberly laid out the quilt top and we all discussed what type of quilting would look best. Sue suggested circles in some areas and that might have been especially effective, except for the fact that my machine is totally hand-guided, and I felt unsure as to whether or not I could quilt perfect circles. Then we decided upon the idea of extending the lines of squares into the negative space and we all agreed it felt like the right thing to do. When I began quilting the top I wanted to soften all the straight lines so I chose swirls and squiggles to add into certain size squares for just that purpose. You'll see one long diagonal going in one direction and all the other lines going the other way. Before I was finished, I took to calling it THE CIRCUIT BOARD QUILT, which really fits the design! I sent Kimberly some pictures of the quilting I had done and we both agreed it simply needed more of the same, so I put it back on the frame and added in extra quilting. We're both very happy how it turned out!

LEFT: MODERN CHAIN A.K.A. THE CIRCUIT BOARD QUILT, detail. Full quilt on page 58.

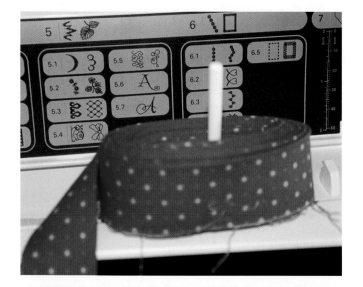

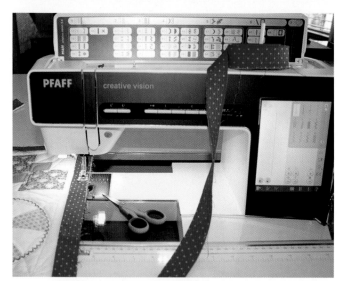

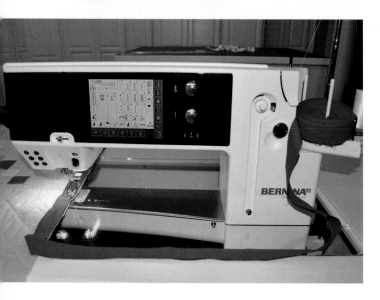

Try This!

Let me show you my super, stress-free method for sewing tangle-free binding to your quilts! After you have made your binding, roll it up neatly and place it on the vertical spool pin on top of your sewing machine.

In the case of my machine, I use the spool to the right to hold the binding while I sew it onto my quilt.

This allows me to easily access just the right amount of binding as I stitch without it falling on the floor, getting tangled up in my chair, or becoming an irresistible cat toy for my furry studio friends!

DRESDEN DAISIES, 64" x 72", designed and made by the author, quilted by Birgit Schüller, Creative BiTS

DRESDEN DAISIES

Finished block sizes:

8" x 8", 16" x 16"

24" x 24"

Skill level:

Skilled Intermediate

Fabric:

Various stripes, geometrics, polka dots

Polka dots, stripes, and geometric and chevron prints make a huge impact when used in a traditional Dresden Plate block in a very non-traditional setting. Simple piecing and fusing make these posies and stem units stitch together quickly and there is lots of room for your own unique interpretation and creative license in this asymmetrical design. I know you're going to love making this one from start to finish!

Some of the fabrics used to make this quilt include: Background, Essential Dots by Moda #8654; Greta Lynn for Kanvas for Benartex Pattern #StripeZone-C 5899; Patrick Lose Mixmasters Dot-to-Dot for Robert Kaufman #7585 yellow and gray, and Simply Color by Vanessa Christenson of V and Co for Moda #10806.

Cut all strips from WOF except as indicated for Fabric #1 in the cutting layout diagram. You may need more or less yardage depending on the size of the stripes and the number of repeats.

FABRIC	YARDS	CUTTING INSTRUCTIONS
#1 – White with small black dots (Background)	4⅜ yards	*Cut the following pieces LOF as shown in the cutting layout diagram (page 70).* • 1 – 24½" x 24½" square • 1 – 14½" x 24½" rectangle • 2 – 16½" x 16½" squares • 1 – 16½" x 72½" rectangle • 1 – 10½" x 24½" rectangle • 1 – 8½" x 16½" rectangle • 26 – 8½" x 8½" squares
#2 – Largest daisy / A (Black/yellow/ red-orange stripe)	1 yard	• Cut 12 – 8" wedges.

(continued)

(continued)

FABRIC	YARDS	CUTTING INSTRUCTIONS
#3 – Daisy B (yellow, black with white dots, black/white stripe, black/gray stripe)	¼ yard each of 4 fabrics	• Cut 5 – 5½" wedges from each of 4 fabrics–20 wedges total.
#4 – Daisy C (yellow dots, black with white dots, black/white stripe)	¼ yard each of 3 fabrics	• Cut 10 – 5½" wedges from yellow dots. • Cut 5 – 5½" from BOTH the black with white dots and black/white stripes—10 wedges total.
#5 – Daisy D (black/ white chevron print, black / gray stripe)	¼ yard each of 2 fabrics	• Cut 10 – 5½" wedges from each of 2 fabrics–20 total wedges.
#6 – Gray with small dots	¼ yard	• Trace 6 stem units onto fusible web from the template (page 77) and fuse to wrong side of fabric.
#7 – Gray with medium dots	½ yard	• Trace 12 stem units onto fusible web from the template (page 77) and fuse to wrong side of fabric.
#8 – Gray geometric	¼ yard	• Trace 8 stem units onto fusible web from the template (page 77) and fuse to wrong side of fabric.
#9 – Daisy centers	scraps	• Trace 1 large and 3 small circles onto fusible web from the templates (page 77). Fuse to the back of fabric scraps and cut out on the drawn line.
Backing	4⅔ yards	• 2 panels 37" x 80"
Batting		• 72" x 80"
Binding	⅝ yard	• Cut 8 – 2¼" strips; piece together to make single-fold, straight-grain binding.

Additional Supplies

EZ Dresden Tool or EZ Fat Cats Tool (optional) or use the
  templates provided (page 77).

Open-toe or appliqué presser foot

4 yards lightweight fusible web

4 yards (temporary) tear-away stabilizer

1 package ⅝" Heavy Duty Wonder-Under Paper Backed Fusible
  Web Tape

Neutral thread for stitching the blocks together.

Monofilament (optional) and coordinating 50-wt. cotton thread
  for machine appliqué

149"

40"

24½" x 24½"	16½" x 72½"											8½" x 16½"	16½" x 16½"	16½" x 16½"	10½" x 24½"
	8½" x 8½"														
14½" x 24½"															

Cutting layout

Choose a striped fabric with stripes running the LOF, parallel to the selvage.

TOP TIP

Stripes, polka dots, chevrons and almost any geometric fabric can really take center stage in this quilt! Don't be afraid to mix and match all kinds of wonky prints to make your daisies and the stems really stand out and be noticed. While you're at it, gather your prettiest contrasting threads to make the machine appliqué accentuate your daisies while using some of your favorite decorative machine stitches. Why not try some satin and scallop stitches to give your flowers an extra flourish? Be sure to check out Try This! (page 75) to learn my favorite technique for stitch stacking!

Construction

Follow these simple steps for preparing striped fabric to accurately cut wedge units for the daisy petals. This method will work for any striped fabric where the stripes run parallel (LOF) to the selvage. It will NOT work for stripes printed from selvage-to-selvage (WOF)!

Lay tool or template (page 77) on an 8" section of the fabric. Use your rotary cutter to cut a small slit in the fabric exactly on the line where you would like the stripe to begin. Be very precise!

Grasp the fabric on either side of the slit and RIP the fabric along the LOF. (I can hear a collective gasp out there, but TRUST ME—this works every single time!)

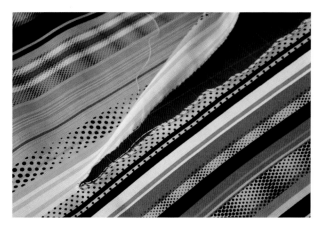

Do not worry about the tiny amount of fraying along the edges. These will disappear by pressing them with a hot iron. Remove the few stray threads that remain.

Tear the stripe all the way to the end of the strip.

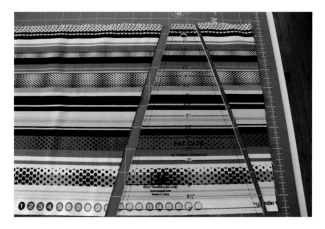

Lay the tool or template on the strip and cut the wedge.

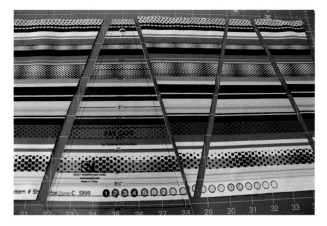

For this quilt you will cut all your wedges (petals) with the stripes going in the same direction.

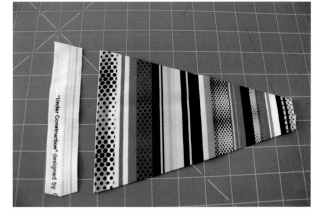

Use the lines on your cutting mat to measure from the small end; trim the wedge so it measures 8" in length.

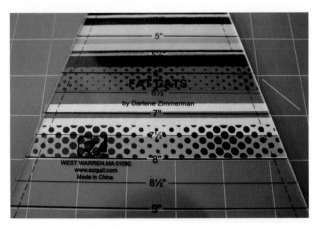

Lay the tool or template on the wedge to make sure it lines up along the 8" line.

Follow this same process for cutting wedges for the three smaller daisies.

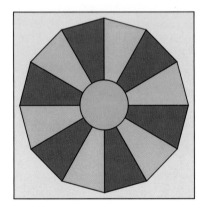

Block 1 – Make 1.

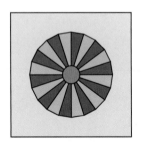

Block 2 – Make 2 on plain background squares.

Block 2 – Make 1 on 4 Stem blocks.

▼ Cut the number of wedges needed for each daisy as listed in the cutting chart.

▼ Lay out the wedges.

▼ Use a scant ¼" seam allowance and stitch wedges together.

▼ You will use 12 – 8" wedges for the large daisy (A) and 20 – 5½" wedges for each of the three small daisies (B, C, and D; 60 total).

▼ Press the seams in the same direction.

▼ Trim the edges prior to adding fusible web to the wrong side of the daisy units. (See the TOP TIP, page 73.)

▼ Fuse the large daisy appliqué to the fabric #1 – 24½" x 24½" background square.

▼ Fuse 2 of the small daisy appliqués to the fabric #1 – 16½" x 16½" background squares.

▼ Set aside the third small daisy appliqué until the Stem blocks are made (page 73).

▼ Fuse the center circle appliqués on top of the completed daisies.

TOP TIP

After sewing wedges together, trim the raw edge points.

Trimming the raw edges at seam intersections ensures the daisy appliqué is round.

Use ⅝" wide fusible tape cut into trapezoid sections to fuse along the inner and outer edges of the wrong side of the daisies.

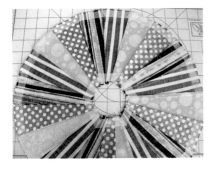

This keeps the appliqué shapes from becoming too stiff yet it holds them in place on the background fabric for machine appliqué.

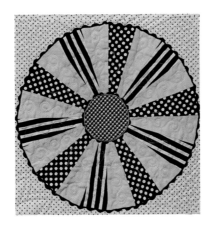

Block 3 – Make 26.

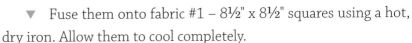
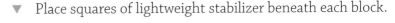

▼ Use the template (page 77) to trace flower stem units as listed in the cutting chart.

▼ Fuse them onto fabric #1 – 8½" x 8½" squares using a hot, dry iron. Allow them to cool completely.

▼ Place squares of lightweight stabilizer beneath each block.

▼ Use a small zigzag stitch (or your favorite machine appliqué stitch) and sew units to background squares.

▼ CAREFULLY remove the stabilizer from the back of your blocks.

Use a small zigzag stitch.

Carefully remove stabilizer.

▼ The Stem blocks should measure 8½" x 8½" unfinished.

▼ Join 4 Stem blocks, orienting them as shown in the quilt assembly diagram.

▼ Fuse the remaining daisy appliqué to the four-block unit.

▼ Fuse the center circle appliqué to the daisy.

▼ Machine appliqué daisies to the background fabric blocks before sewing the quilt top together. (See Try This! on pages 75–76 for my fabulous Stitch Stacking technique!)

▼ Stitch blocks together according to the quilt assembly diagram (below).

▼ Quilt, bind, add a label and enjoy!

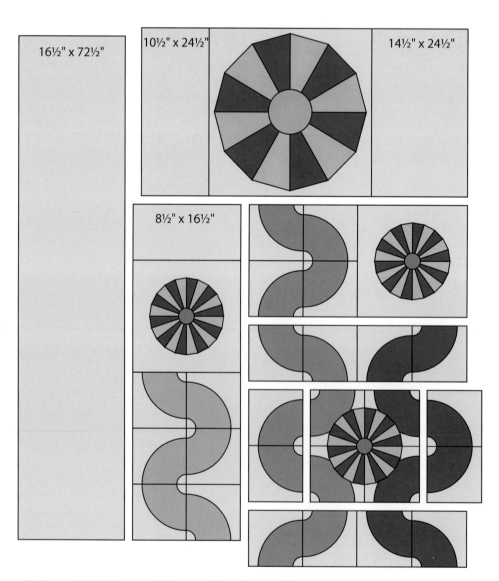

Quilt assembly. Background piece cut dimensions are shown.

Thoughts about the Quilting from Birgit

These funky daisies called for some funky quilting. First, I quilted the pieced flower blossoms just enough to tack them down. Stitching in the ditch around the circles and the stems added some definition. For the stems, I used a spiky triangular quilting motif because I felt it was suitable. In the large, open background areas I used my large Spine-flex templates by Westalee Designs from Australia to add more flowers and to break down the background areas into sections that were easier to work with. I subdivided these sections further into odd-shaped portions that I filled with parallel lines. I changed the orientation of the parallel lines from section to section.

For the pieced daisies and background flowers I used threads in the yellows and yellow-orange. The stems were quilted with gray thread and for the background quilting I used cream colored thread. I think the quilting added the perfect amount of modern design and whimsy to an eye-catching quilt!

Try This!

For a fabulous machine-appliqué finish to your daisies, use your sewing machine and try my easy technique of Stitch Stacking! Quite simply, you layer basic decorative or utility stitches next to or on top of each other with contrasting threads to make them stand out and accentuate your fabrics perfectly! In essence, you are creating unique and completely new decorative stitches. Here's how:

LEFT: DRESDEN DAISIES, detail. Full quilt on page 67.

modern QUILTS & more ••••• KIMBERLY einmo

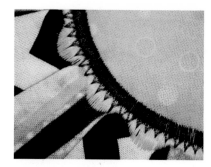

I used 50-wt. black thread and stitched a wide and dense satin stitch around this daisy center. Then I used 28-wt. yellow cotton thread and topstitched a zigzag that was slightly less wide and with a longer stitch length to add a pop of color.

I used 50-wt. black thread and a wide, dense satin stitch for the inner ring around the center. Then I used 50-wt. yellow cotton thread to sew a decorative scallop stitch outside the inner black ring. I used a 28-wt. black cotton thread to topstitch a zigzag overlapping the scallop stitch.

For this daisy center, I used 50-wt. black cotton thread to sew a decorative scallop stitch topped off with 28-wt. yellow cotton thread and a triple straight stitch along the inside edge of the scallop stitch.

LEFT: Stitch stacking isn't just for the daisy centers. Create your own stitches around the outside edges of your daisies, too. I used 50-wt. black cotton thread to sew a decorative oval stitch. Then I top-stitched a triple straight stitch directly through the middle of the ovals with a 28-wt. yellow cotton thread. This gives the illusion of the stitches being cleverly tied in bunches for a smashing edge finish.

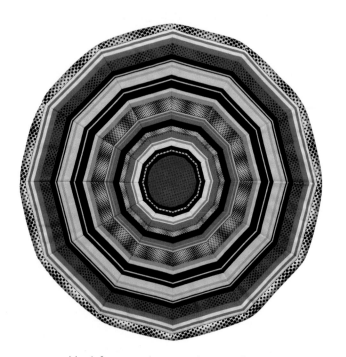

Use leftover wedges to make a candle mat!

Round 2 Re-do: CANDLE MAT

After I finished cutting wedges with the EZ Fat Cats Tool from my striped fabrics, I discovered I had a few wedges left over. It only took me about an hour to sew the wedges together, add a very light batting and backing, and turn it inside out to create a sweet little candle mat. I quilted it with black thread following the lines of the stripes for an ultra fast finish! If you need a gift in a hurry, this is it!

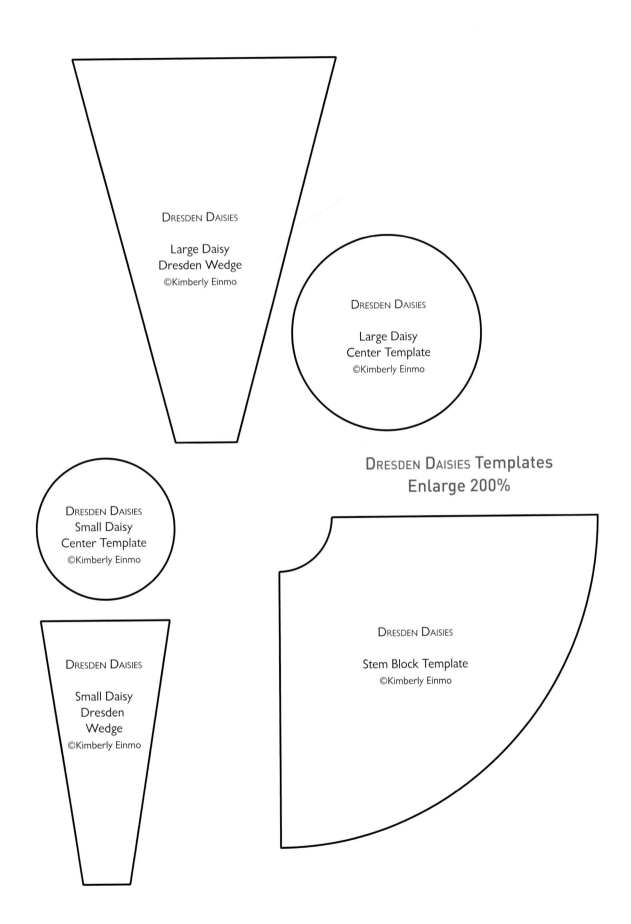

DRESDEN DAISIES

Large Daisy
Dresden Wedge
©Kimberly Einmo

DRESDEN DAISIES

Large Daisy
Center Template
©Kimberly Einmo

DRESDEN DAISIES Templates
Enlarge 200%

DRESDEN DAISIES
Small Daisy
Center Template
©Kimberly Einmo

DRESDEN DAISIES

Small Daisy
Dresden
Wedge
©Kimberly Einmo

DRESDEN DAISIES

Stem Block Template
©Kimberly Einmo

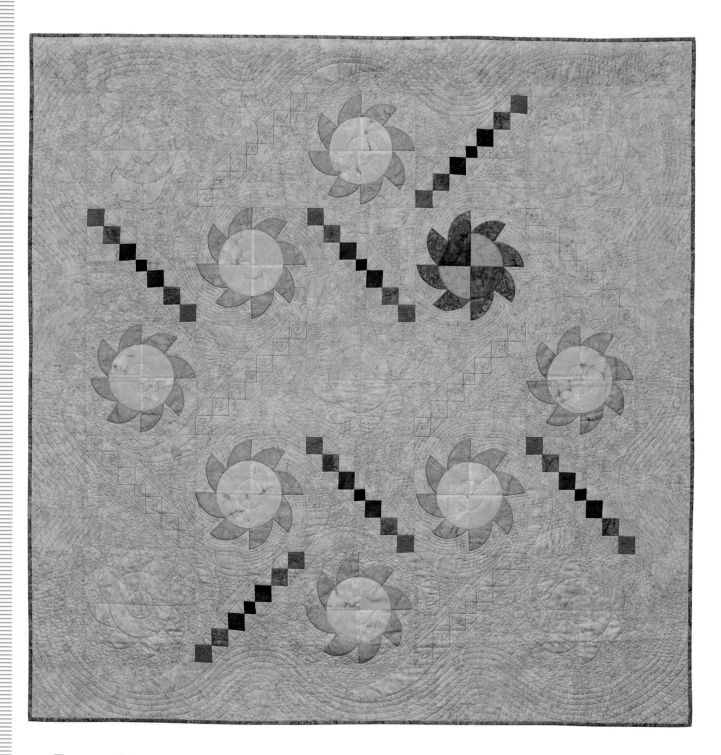

FLOWER POWER, 60" x 60", designed by the author, made and quilted by Christine LaCroix, Quilt Patch Deco Quilting

FLOWER POWER

W ho says modern can't be cheerfully charming at the same time? The simplicity of this sweet quilt is beautifully enhanced by the complementary colors and the texture of the quilting. The appliquéd flowers and pieced Modified Chain blocks combine whimsical with a touch of traditional to create a quilt that is adorable, fresh, and new. Fusing makes the process fast and fun, and you'll have a fanciful quilt in no time.

Skill level:

Skilled Beginner

Fabric:

Timeless Treasures Java Blenders. All colors listed in the fabric chart are from the #B7900 line.

Cut all strips from WOF except as indicated for fabric #1 in the cutting layout diagram (page 80).

FABRIC	YARDS	CUTTING INSTRUCTIONS
#1 – Lilac (Background)	3⅜ yards	*Cut the following pieces from LOF as shown in the cutting layout diagram (page 80).* • 2 – 5½" x 60½" strips (top and bottom borders) • 2 – 5½" x 50½" strips (side borders) • 1 – 10½" x 30½" rectangle • 4 – 10½" x 20½" rectangles • 8 – 10½" x 10½" squares • 12 – 5" x 6" rectangles • 1 – 5" x 40" strip, cut in half across the width *From the remaining yardage, cut WOF:* • 2 – 3½" x 40" strips • 1 – 2" x 40" strip, cut in half across the width
#2 – Halo (Light yellow)	¼ yard	• Cut 2 – 3½" strips.
#3 – Daffodil (Medium yellow)	¼ yard	• Cut 2 – 3½" strips.
#4 – Pollen (Gold)	½ yard	(Petals are cut later.)
#5 – Asparagus (Light green)	⅛ yard	• Cut 2 – 3½" x 3½" squares.

(continued)

(continued)

FABRIC	YARDS	CUTTING INSTRUCTIONS
#6 – Avocado (Medium green)	⅛ yard	• Cut 2 – 3½" x 3½" squares.
#7 – Peridot (Olive green)	⅛ yard	(Petals are cut later.)
#8 – Eggplant (Dark purple)	⅛ yard	• Cut 1 – 1½" x 40" strip.
#9 – Potion (Medium dark purple)	⅛ yard	• Cut 1 – 2" x 40" strip.
#10 – Violet (Medium purple)	⅛ yard	• Cut 1 – 2" x 40" strip.
#11 – Petunia (Light purple)	⅛ yard	• Cut 1 – 2" x 40" strip.
Backing	4 yards	• 2 panels 34" x 68"
Batting		• 68" x 68"
Binding	½ yard	• Cut 7 – 2¼" strips; piece together to make single-fold, straight-grain binding.

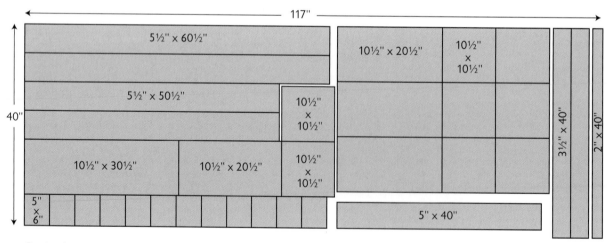

Cutting layout

Construction

▼ Sew a fabric #8 – 1½" strip between two halves of a fabric #1 – 5" strip. (Save the remaining fabric for another project.)

▼ Press the seams toward the fabric #8 strip.

▼ Cut 6 – 1½" units.

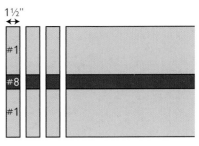

Make 1.   Cut 6.

▼ Sew a fabric #9 – 2" strip and a fabric #1 – 3½" strip.

▼ Press the seam toward the fabric #9 strip.

▼ Cut 12 – 2" units.

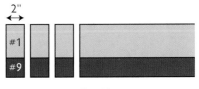

Make 1.   Cut 12.

▼ Sew a fabric #11 – 2" strip and a fabric #1 – 3½" strip.

▼ Press the seam toward the fabric #11 strip.

▼ Cut 12 – 2" units.

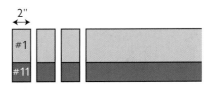

Make 1.   Cut 12.

▼ Sew a fabric #10 – 2" strip between two halves of a fabric #1 – 2" strip. (Save the remaining fabric for another project.)

▼ Press the seams toward the fabric #10 strip.

▼ Cut 12 – 2" units.

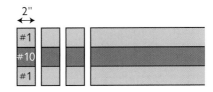

Make 1.   Cut 12.

▼ Assemble Small blocks using the units you just constructed.

▼ Make 12 Small blocks measuring 5" x 5" unfinished.

Make 12 Small blocks.

▼ Assemble the modified Modified Chain blocks using the small blocks, 1½" units, and fabric #1 – 5" x 6" rectangles.

▼ Press the seams as shown by the arrows.

▼ The blocks should measure 10½" x 10½" unfinished.

▼ Make 6 blocks.

▼ Make 2 strip-sets with the 3½" fabric #2 and #3 strips. Cut 14 segments from each strip-set.

▼ Join pairs of segments to make 7 four-patch units.

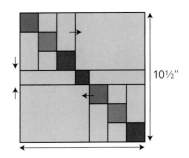

Make 6 Modified Chain blocks.

3½"

Cut 14.   Make 2.

Make 7.

Make 1.

Trim four-patch circles on the drawn line.

Make 7.

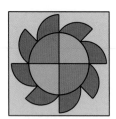

Make 1.

▼ Sew 2 fabric #6 – 3½" x 3½" squares and 2 fabric #5 – 3½" x 3½" squares together to make a four-patch unit to measure 6½" x 6½" unfinished.

▼ Using the 6" template (page 85), trace 8 circles onto fusible web. Cut the circles slightly outside the drawn lines.

▼ Use a hot iron to fuse the circles on the wrong side of the four-patch units.

▼ Trim the four-patch circles on the drawn line.

▼ Trace 64 petal shapes (page 83) onto the paper side of the fusible web. Cut slightly outside the drawn lines. Fuse 56 to the wrong side of fabric #4 and the remaining 8 to the wrong side of fabric #7. Cut out on the drawn lines.

▼ Carefully arrange the petal edges underneath the circle four-patch units on fabric #1 – 10½" x 10½" squares as shown.

TOP TIP

Fold your background squares in quarters and press. Use the fold lines to align the four-patch circle seams and petals.

▼ Use a hot iron and fuse the petals in place.

▼ Using temporary tear-away stabilizer underneath each block; machine appliqué the raw edges of the fused shapes.

▼ Carefully remove all stabilizer from the back of each block after completing machine appliqué.

▼ Arrange the blocks according to the quilt assembly diagram (page 83). Join the blocks into rows. Sew the rows together to complete the quilt top.

▼ Quilt, bind, add a label, and enjoy!

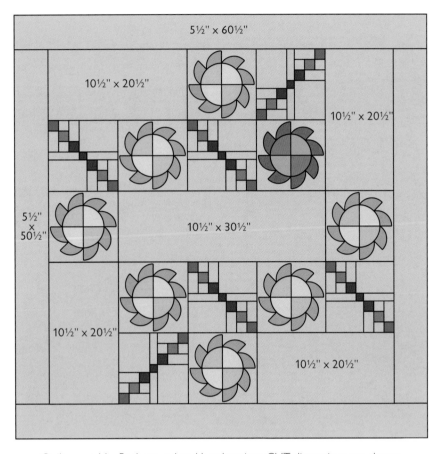

Quilt assembly. Background and border piece CUT dimensions are shown.

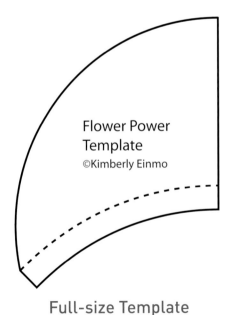

Flower Power
Template
©Kimberly Einmo

Full-size Template

Thoughts about the Quilting from Christine

I loved making this quilt! I love the original design and the fabrics Kimberly chose for me to piece, appliqué, and quilt this quilt from beginning to end! When I came to the quilting stage with my APQS Millennium machine, I wanted to give the impression of movement and flow, and with the precious help and suggestion of my husband, Joseph, decided to repeat the appliqué designs and the squares in the open spaces of the background fabric. I used a dark purple shiny thread from Embrofil to trace the squares, and I quilted a portion of light purple with Embrofil in

the background with a point going to the right to emphasize the movement behind the four central flowers. I also quilted some irregular lines that I repeated in the borders to accentuate the modern feeling of this quilt. I love the way it turned out!

Try This! The Odd Truth about Borders

Years ago, a very wise and talented quilting instructor told me there is a distinct difference between homemade and handmade. She said homemade looks like something made by someone without much talent or taste. (Ouch.) On the other hand, handmade looks like "something exquisitely made by talented hands meant to be treasured." I never forgot her advice and I promised myself I would strive to make things that look handmade.

She went on to explain one of the ways you can spot a quilt that looks homemade is by the borders. A homemade quilt has borders made from widths cut from even numbers (for instance, 4", 6", 10", and so on.) But a handmade quilt has borders with widths cut from odd fabric widths (like 3", 5", 7", and so on.) There is something about an odd-size border width that is pleasing to the viewer; the eye perceives it as attractive and proportionate instead of chunky and clunky. Most modern quilts do not have borders but as you will see, many of the quilts in this book have the negative space extended because I added borders cut from background fabric. In most cases, you'll find they have odd number border widths and I think this makes all the difference to the viewer's eye. So remember, handmade is good. Homemade? Not so much.

RIGHT: FLOWER POWER, detail. Full quilt on page 78.

FLOWER POWER

6"
Center Template
©Kimberly Einmo

FLOWER POWER 6" Template
Full size

T's, 48" x 56", designed by the author, made by Claire Neal, Newport News, Virginia, quilted by Birgit Schüller, Creative BiTS

T's

Tblocks are inherently traditional, so I challenged myself to design a thoroughly modern quilt using them. With the help of my Electric Quilt (EQ7) software I played with various design options and auditioned all sorts of unique and clever layouts. Ultimately, I knew I wanted an asymmetrical design with lots of negative space, but I also wanted the T block to be easily recognizable. I think this design strikes the perfect note of harmony between traditional and modern, and the free-form flying geese quilting adds just the right amount of depth and movement.

Instructions for the traditional method are listed in RED. Instructions for using the EZ Flying Geese Ruler are listed in BLUE. Everything listed in BLACK applies to both methods. Background fabrics are cut LOF. Cut all strips WOF.

Finished block size:
  8" x 8"
Skill level:
  Skilled Intermediate
Fabric:
  Timeless Treasures Java
  Blenders and various batiks
  from my stash

Additional Supplies

EZ Flying Geese Ruler (optional)

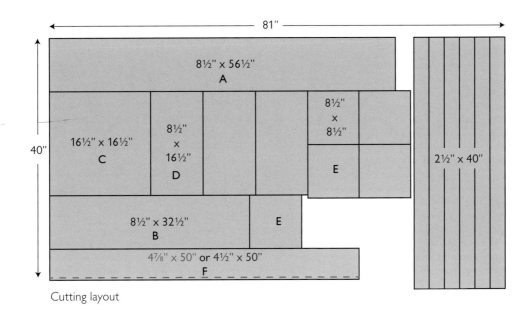

Cutting layout

FABRIC	YARDS	CUTTING INSTRUCTIONS
#1 – Background	2½ yards	Cut the following pieces from yardage LOF as shown in the cutting layout diagram (page 87). • 1 – 8½" x 56½" rectangle (A) • 1 – 8½" x 32½" rectangle (B) • 1 – 16½" x 16½" square (C) • 3 – 8½" x 16½" rectangles (D) • 5 – 8½" x 8½" squares (E) • 1 – 4⅞" x 50" strip (F); subcut 8 – 4⅞" x 4⅞" squares. Cut 1x diagonally to yield 16 triangles. • 1 – 4½" x 50" strip (F); subcut 18 – 4½" Side B triangles Cut the following pieces from yardage WOF. • Cut 8 – 2½" strips; subcut 64 – 2½" x 4½" rectangles. • Cut 6 – 2½" strips; subcut 64 – 2½" Side A triangles.
#2 – Blue/white print	⅜ yard	• Cut 2 – 4½" strips; subcut 12 – 4½" x 4½" squares.
#3 – Medium blue	¼ yard	• Cut 2 – 2½" strips; subcut 24 – 2½" x 2½" squares. • Cut 1 – 2½" strip; fold strips RST and cut 12 pairs – 2½" Side B triangles.
#4 – Medium/dark blue	¼ yard	• Cut 2 – 2½" strips; subcut 24 – 2½" x 2½" squares. • Cut 1 – 2½" strip; fold strips RST and cut 12 pairs – 2½" Side B triangles.
#5 – Dark blue	½ yard	• Cut 2 – 4⅞" strips; subcut 6 – 4⅞" x4⅞" squares. Cut 1x diagonally to yield 12 triangles. • Cut 3 – 2½" strips; subcut 48 – 2½" x 2½" squares. • Cut 1 – 4½" strip; subcut 12 – 4½" Side B triangles. • Cut 2 – 2½" strips; fold strips RST and cut 24 pairs – 2½" Side B triangles.
#6 – Light green	⅛ yard	• Cut 1 – 2½" strip; subcut 8 – 2½" x 2½" squares. • Fold strip RST and cut 4 pairs – 2½" Side B triangles.
#7 – Medium/light green	⅛ yard	• Cut 1 – 2½" strip; subcut 8 – 2½" x 2½" squares. • Fold strip RST and cut 4 pairs – 2½" Side B triangles.
#8 – Bright olive green	¼ yard	• Cut 1 – 4⅞" strip; subcut 1 – 4⅞" x 4⅞" square. Cut 1x diagonally to yield 2 triangles. Trim remainder of the strip to 2½"; subcut 8 – 2½" x 2½" squares. • Cut 1 – 4½" strip; subcut 2 – 4½" Side B triangles. Trim remainder of the strip to 2½" and fold RST; subcut 4 pairs – 2½" Side B triangles.

(continued)

(continued)

FABRIC	YARDS	CUTTING INSTRUCTIONS
#9 – Dark blue green	¼ yard	• Cut 1 – 4⅞" strip; subcut 1 – 4⅞" x 4⅞" square. Cut 1x diagonally to yield 2 triangles. Trim remainder of the strip to 2½"; subcut 8 – 2½" x 2½" squares. • Cut 1 – 4½" strip; subcut 2 – 4½" Side B triangles. Trim remainder of the strip to 2½" and fold RST; subcut 4 pairs – 2½" Side B triangles.
#10 – Light green print	¼ yard	• Cut 1 – 4½" strip; subcut 4 – 4½" x 4½" squares.
Backing	3¾ yards	• 2 panels 28" x 64"
Batting		• 56" x 64"
Binding	½ yard	• Cut 7 – 2¼" strips; piece together to make single-fold, straight-grain binding.

Construction

Traditional HST method (page 16)

▼ To make HSTs, combine fabrics #1/#5 triangles cut from 4⅞" squares. Make 12.

▼ Stitch ¼" from raw edge of triangle units.

▼ Press the seam allowances toward the darker fabric.

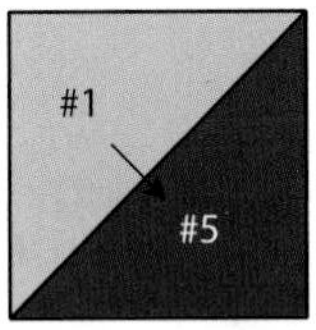

Make 12 – #1/#5 HSTs.

EZ Flying Geese HST method (page 15)

▼ To make HSTs, place fabrics #1/#5 – 4½" Side B triangles RST.

▼ Stitch ¼" from raw edge of triangle units. Press the seam toward the darker fabric.

▼ HSTs should measure 4½" x 4½" unfinished. Make 12 – #1/#5 HSTs.

▼ In the same manner, make 2 – #1/#8 and 2 – #1/#9 HSTs.

▼ Press the seams away from the fabric #1 triangles.

▼ HST units should measure 4½" x 4½" unfinished.

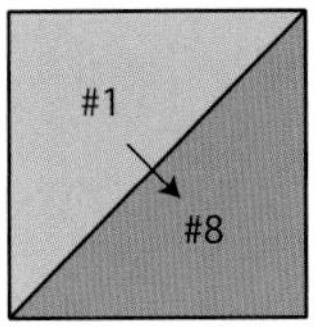

Make 2 – #1/#8 HSTs.

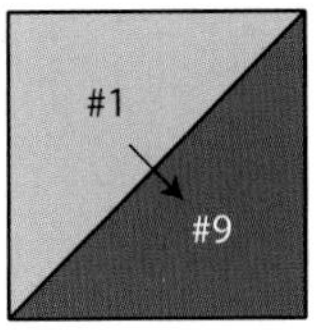

Make 2 – #1/#9 HSTs.

Make 12 of each version using #1 Side A triangles and fabrics #3/#5 Side B triangles.

Make 12 of each version using #1 Side A triangles and fabrics #4/#5 Side B triangles.

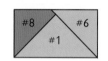

Make 2 of each version using #1 Side A triangles and fabrics #6/#8 Side B triangles.

Make 2 of each version using #1 Side A triangles and fabrics #7/#8 Side B triangles.

Make 2 of each version using #1 Side A triangles and fabrics #6/#9 Side B triangles.

Make 2 of each version using #1 Side A triangles and fabrics #7/#9 Side B triangles.

Flying Geese Assembly

▼ Follow directions on page 16 to make flying geese units using the traditional method.

▼ Follow directions on page 16 to make flying geese units using the EZ Flying Geese Ruler method.

▼ ALWAYS press the seams toward the side triangles. Don't forget to trim all the dog ears!

▼ Flying geese units should measure 2½" x 4½" unfinished.

TOP TIP

As you construct the flying geese units, regardless of the method, be sure to take the time to measure each unit and trim any excess fabric or dog ears before sewing them into the blocks. By removing any uneven areas or "wonky bits" from the units, you'll ensure that your T blocks will stitch together with crisp points that will lie flat. In the long run, you'll save lots of time and frustration. *Truly!*

▼ Construct the flying geese units as shown.

▼ Press the seams in the direction of the side triangles.

▼ The flying geese units should measure 2½" x 4½" unfinished.

▼ Using the HSTs, flying geese units, and 4½" x 4½" squares, assemble the T blocks as shown.

▼ The blocks should measure 8½" x 8½" unfinished.

▼ Arrange the blocks and background pieces according to the quilt assembly diagram (below). Join the blocks into columns as shown. Sew the columns together to complete the quilt top.

▼ Quilt, bind, add a label, and enjoy!

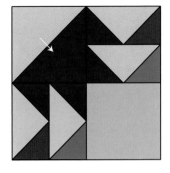

Make 12 blue T blocks.

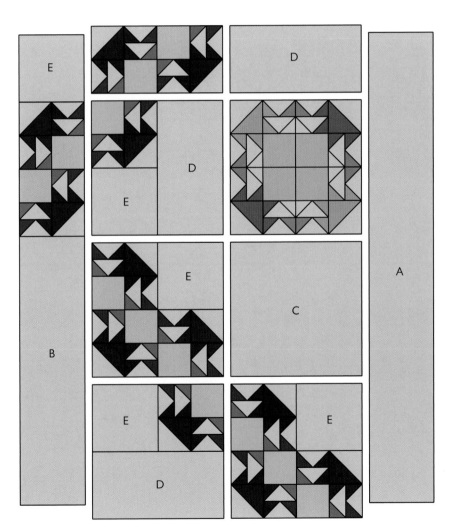

Quilt assembly

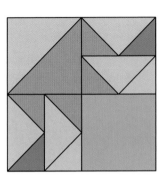

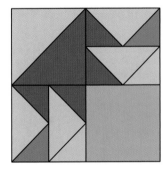

Make 2 blocks of each version of green T blocks.

Thoughts about the Quilting from Birgit

This top features a very traditional block in an extremely modern layout. Trying to carry this concept into the quilting, I quilted the individual blocks as I would have done in a traditional setting using some continuous, swirly designs, loops, and continuous curves. However, for filling the open background spaces, I left traditional quilting behind and quilted a line of curved flying geese meandering in between the different block clusters using a light-colored thread to match the light blue background fabric. To add more definition to the geese, I added simple shapes and small-scale background quilting between the geese and the T block clusters. The result is an effective use of the negative space, adding interest and texture without distracting from the overall unique design. Perfect!

TRY THIS! The Proper Way to Add a Hanging Sleeve

As a quilt judge, I have the opportunity to see many beautiful quilts hung on display. Sadly, sometimes their beauty is distorted because of a poorly attached hanging sleeve. Many quilters make the mistake of sewing the sleeve flush against the quilt back without leaving any room for the rod or pole to be inserted. Fortunately, this is an easy thing to correct.

The hanging sleeve should be at least 4" (finished), but be sure to check the rules for each contest where you may enter your quilt. Hand stitch (you certainly don't want any stitches from your sewing machine to show on the front) the sleeve in place along the top of the quilt, just below the binding. When you get ready to stitch the opposite edge of the sleeve, lay a yardstick, dowel, or your Strip Stick underneath the sleeve along the edge already sewn. Smooth the sleeve into position, pin in place, and hand stitch to finish.

This ensures some "ease" in the sleeve for the rod or pole so the quilt will hang flat, almost as if it is hanging invisibly!

LEFT: T's, detail. Full quilt on page 86.

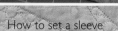

How to set a sleeve

RETRO RED STAR, 70" x 84", designed by the author, made by Stevii Graves, Leesburg, Virginia, quilted by Birgit Schüller, Creative BiTS

RETRO RED STAR

Finished block size:

14" x 14"

Skill level:

Skilled Beginner

Fabric:

Timeless Treasures Java Blenders (All colors listed in fabric chart #B7900)

M odern, masculine, with a touch of retro thrown in for good measure, plus the added element of surprise with the red star! Think Southern California architecture or concrete block walls in the late '50s. But classic styles come back around and everything old is mod again! This large quilt will look fabulous in any modern style bedroom or would make a powerful statement hanging in an entryway of a residence with a minimalist style. Depending on the colors you choose to make your version, it could look brassy and bold or restrained and refined. Either way, this design totally rocks the modern element.

Instructions for the traditional method are listed in RED. Instructions for using the EZ Flying Geese Ruler are listed in BLUE. Everything listed in BLACK applies to both methods. Background fabrics are cut LOF. All other strips are cut WOF.

FABRIC	YARDS	CUTTING INSTRUCTIONS
#1 – Background (Air)	4 yards	Cut the following units from yardage LOF as shown in the cutting layout diagram (page 95). • Cut 1 – 14½" x 84½" rectangle. • Cut 1 – 14½" x 42½" rectangle. • Cut 2 – 2½" strips; subcut 25 – 2½" x 2½" squares. • Cut 5 – 6½" x 42" strips; subcut 80 – 2½" x 6½" rectangles . From WOF, cut: • 6 – 4½" strips (5 for the #1/#3 strip-sets, 1 for the #1/#4 strip-set). • 10 – 2½" strips (for the #1/#2 strip-sets).
#2 – Yellow (Pollen)	1¼ yards	• Cut 16 – 2½" strips (15 for strip-sets). • Subcut 1 strip into 4 – 2½" x 4½" rectangles (for block C).

(continued)

(continued)

FABRIC	YARDS	CUTTING INSTRUCTIONS
#3 – Green (Emerald)	1¼ yards	• Cut 11 – 2½" strips. • Subcut one strip into 4 – 2½" x 4½" rectangles and 4 – 2½" x 2½" squares. Set aside the remaining strips for the strip-sets.
#4 – Red (Crimson)	¾ yard	• Cut 1 – 2½" strip; subcut 8 – 2½" x 2½" squares. Set aside the remaining #4 half strip. • Cut 1 – 2½" strip and pair with a fabric #1 – 2½". • Subcut 8 – 2½" x 3¼" rectangles for the HSTs. • Subcut 16 – 2½" Side B triangle pairs for the HSTs.
Backing	5½ yards	• 2 panels 39" x 92"
Batting		• 78" x 92"
Binding (Pollen)	⅝ yard	• Cut 8 – 2¼" strips for binding; piece together to make single-fold, straight-of-grain binding.

Additional Supplies

EZ Flying Geese Ruler (optional)

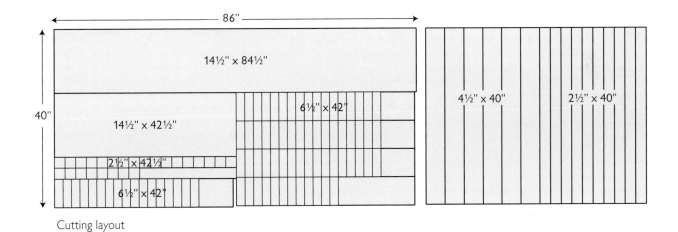

Cutting layout

Construction

Make 16 – #1/#4 HSTs.

Traditional HST method (page 16)

▼ Combine fabrics #1/#4 – 2½" x 3¼" rectangles RST.

▼ Stitch on drawn diagonal lines and trim in the middle of the sewn lines.

▼ Press the seam allowances toward the darker fabric.

EZ Flying Geese method (page 15)

▼ Stitch ¼" from the raw edge of the Side B triangle pairs; press the seam toward the darker fabric.

▼ HSTs should measure 2½" x 2½" unfinished.

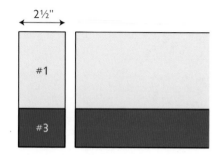

Cut 80.   Make 5.

▼ Make 5 strip-sets with fabric #1 – 4½" strips and fabric #3 – 2½" strips.

▼ Press the seams toward #3.

▼ Cut 80 – 2½" units.

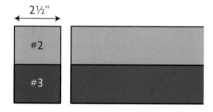

Cut 80.   Make 5.

▼ Make 5 strip-sets with fabric #2 – 2½" strips and fabric #3 – 2½" strips.

▼ Press the seams toward #2.

▼ Cut 80 – 2½" units.

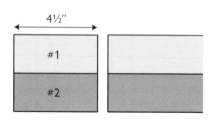

Cut 76.   Make 10.

▼ Make 10 strip-sets with fabric #1 – 2½" strips and fabric #2 – 2½" strips.

▼ Press the seams toward #2.

▼ Cut 76 – 4½" units.

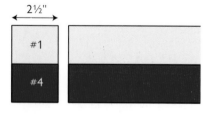

Make 1.   Cut 4.

▼ Make 1 strip-set with the remaining #4 – 2½" half-strip and half of a #1 – 4½" strip.

▼ Press the seams toward #4.

▼ Cut 4 – 2½" units.

Assemble the Blocks

For each Block A you will need:

▲ 1 – #1 – 2½" x 2½" square (for the center)
▲ 4 – #1 – 2½" x 6½" rectangles
▲ 4 – #1/#3 – 2½" x 6½" rectangle units
▲ 4 – #1/#2 – 4½" x 4½" square units
▲ 4 – #2/#3 – 2½" x 4½" rectangle units

▼ The block should measure 14½" x 14½" unfinished.

▼ Make 16 blocks.

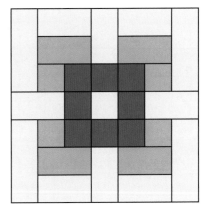

Block A – Make 16.

For Block B you will need:

▲ 1 – #1 – 2½" x 2½" square (for the center)
▲ 4 – #1 – 2½" x 6½" rectangles
▲ 4 – #1/#4 – 2½" x 6½" rectangle units
▲ 4 – #1/#3 – 4½" x 4½" square units
▲ 4 – #3/#4 – 2½" x 4½" rectangle units

▼ The block should measure 14½" x 14½" unfinished.

▼ Make 1 block.

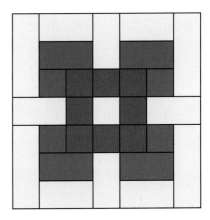

Block B – Make 1.

For each Block C you will need:

▲ 2 – #1 – 2½" squares (for the center and corner)
▲ 3 – #1 – 2½" x 6½" rectangles
▲ 4 – #1/#3 – 2½" x 6½" rectangle units
▲ 3 – #1/#2 – 4½" x 4½" square units
▲ 1 – #2 – 2½" x 4½" rectangle
▲ 4 – #2/#3 – 2½" x 4½" rectangle units
▲ 4 – #1/#4 – 2½" x 2½" HSTs

▼ The block should measure 14½" x 14½" unfinished.

▼ Make 4 blocks.

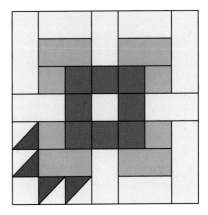

Block C – Make 4.

▼ Arrange the blocks and background rectangles according to the quilt assembly diagram (page 98). Join the blocks into sections as shown. Sew the sections together to complete the quilt top.

▼ Quilt, bind, add a label, and enjoy!

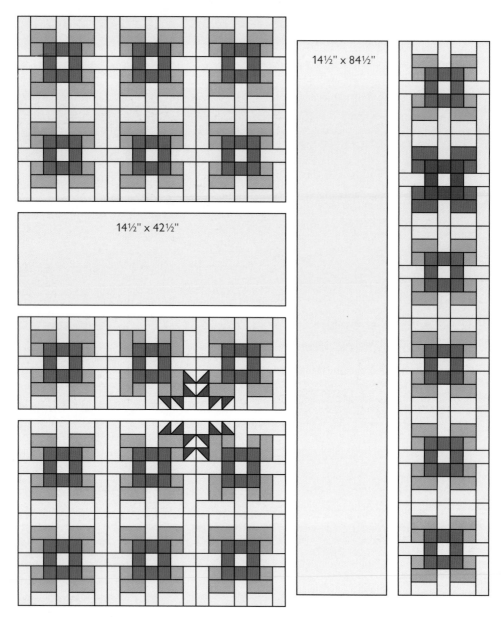

14½" x 42½"

14½" x 84½"

Quilt assembly

Thoughts about the Quilting from Birgit

For this very geometric and thus very masculine quilt I avoided ANY whimsical quilting. In between and inside the quilted blocks I quilted straight lines with matching thread colors to dominate the quilt surface. Just a few yellow stitching lines extend from the pieced blocks into the background. The pieced red star and the one green block attract enough attention by their own design, so the quilting didn't have to emphasize this any further. Instead, I felt that the overall geometry of the quilt needed to be carried into the open background areas. Thus, I recreated the pieced block design in these areas and quilted them accordingly, using thread that matched the color of the background fabric—strong, dynamic and effective.

Try This! A Change of Colors Makes a Bold Statement

The design of this quilt makes it the perfect gift for the hard-to-buy-for man in your life. To make it even more masculine, why not consider a black/gray/lime green color scheme? Or black, gray, and red! This quilt is easy to construct and will look great made with solid, batik, or almost any printed fabrics. You can't go wrong with this dynamic layout and the color combo possibilities are endless. Enough said. Now, go quilt!

RIGHT: RETRO RED STAR, detail. Full quilt on page 93.

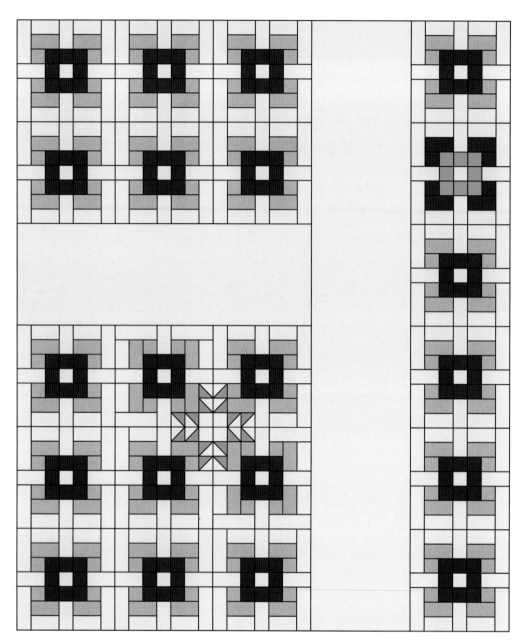

Alternate color option

SATURATED COLOR PLAY, 57" x 57", designed and made by the author,
quilted by Carolyn Archer, Ohio Star Quilting

SATURATED COLOR PLAY

Finished block size:
9" x 9"
Skill level:
Skilled Beginner
Fabric:
Timeless Treasures Java Blenders plus various batiks from my stash

The pieced blocks of this quilt are purely traditional. Even the layout tends to be traditional by design. But what makes this quilt modern is the balance of saturated color and *avant-garde* machine quilting designs. If you love color, you'll absolutely love making this quilt.

Selecting the colors and fabrics was half the fun! I played with stacks of richly hued batiks for several days until I finally found the perfect arrangement based on a design layout I had created in grayscale in EQ7. I think you'll learn a lot about the principles of the color wheel and about your own reaction to colors as you construct this striking, modern quilt!

Cut all strips WOF.

FABRIC	YARDS	CUTTING INSTRUCTIONS
#1 – Light blue/green mottled batik (For background)	1¾ yards	• Cut 4 – 9½" strips; subcut 44 – 3½" x 9½" rectangles. • Cut 1 – 6½" strip; subcut 8 – 3½" x 6½" rectangles. • Cut 4 – 3½" strips; subcut 36 – 3½" x 3½" squares.
#2 – Multi-color batik (Timeless Treasures XTonga B9386 – Taffy)	1¼ yards	• Cut 1 – 9½" x 9½" square. • Cut 8 – 1½" strips. • Cut 6 – 2¼" strips; piece together to make single-fold, straight-grain binding.
#3 – Orange, Pink, Blue, Yellow Green	⅛ yard EACH of 4 fabrics	• Cut 1 – 3½" strip from each of the 4 colors; subcut 7 – 3½" x 3½" squares (total 28 squares).
#4 – Peach, Violet, Turquoise, Mint Green	⅛ yard EACH of 4 fabrics	• Cut 2 – 1½" strips from each of the 4 colors (total 8 strips).

(continued)

(continued)

FABRIC	YARDS	CUTTING INSTRUCTIONS
#5 – Yellow, Red, Purple, Green	⅓ yard EACH of 4 fabrics	• Cut 3 – 9½" x 9½" squares from each of the 4 colors (total 12 squares).
#6 – Indigo	¼ yard	• Cut 2 – 1½" strips.
Backing	3¾ yards	• 2 panels 33" x 65"
Batting		• 65" x 65"

TOP TIP

This is a really fun quilt to make but it takes a bit of color planning before you ever put your rotary cutter to fabric. My inspiration came from my fabric #2, the multicolored fabric in the center, and I chose all the other batiks based on that fabric. I wanted my quilt to informally mirror the color wheel, so I spent time laying the fabrics out to get the perfect flow of colors around the color wheel. Then I made sure to assign each fabric a number so I wouldn't get confused and cut them incorrectly. Once you have your fabrics laid out, it is helpful to take a digital photo of them as I did so you can refer to it for proper color placement.

Construction

Block 1

▼ Using (2) 3½" x 3½" squares and (2) – 3½" x 6½" rectangles of fabric #1 and (3) 3½" x 3½" squares of one #3 fabric color, construct the blocks as shown.

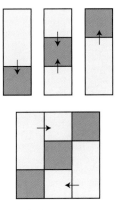

Block 1 construction

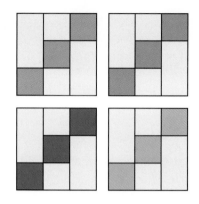

Make 1 block in each of 3 remaining colors.

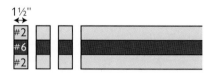

1½"

#2
#6
#2

Make 2 strip-sets. Cut 32 units.

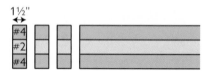

1½"

#4
#2
#4

Make 1 strip-set in each color. Cut 16 units (64 total).

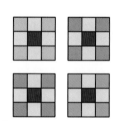

Make 8 each #4 color (32 total).

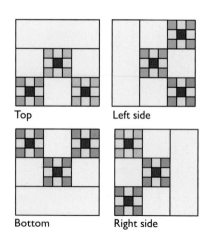

Top   Left side

Bottom   Right side

Make 1 block in each of 4 colors.

▼ Make 1 block for each of the 3 remaining fabric #3 colors as shown. The blocks should measure 9½" x 9½" unfinished.

Block 2

▼ Make 2 strip-sets, each with 2 fabric #2 – 1½" strips and 1 fabric #6 – 1½" strip.

▼ Press the seams toward fabric #6.

▼ Cut 32 – 1½" units.

▼ Make 1 strip-set in each of 4 fabric #4 colors, with 2 fabric #4 – 1½" strips and 1 fabric #2 – 1½" strip each.

▼ Press the seams toward fabric #4.

▼ Cut 16 – 1½" units from each strip-set (64 total).

▼ Combine the units to form 3½" x 3½" unfinished nine-patch units.

▼ Make 8 nine-patch units from each of 4 fabric #4 colors.

Block 3

▼ Make 1 block in each of 4 color combinations as shown with 3 – 3½" squares, 1 – 3½" x 9½" rectangle of fabric #1, and 3 – 3½" x 3½" nine-patch units (Block 2). Pay careful attention to the color combinations and placement of the nine-patch units within the blocks to make the quilt's secondary design appears.

▼ The blocks should measure 9½" x 9½" unfinished.

Block 4

▼ Make 1 block in each of 4 colors as shown with 3 – 3½" x 3½" nine-patch units (Block 2), 2 matching 3½" squares of fabric #3, and 4 – 3½" squares of fabric #1.

▼ Press the seams in direction of arrows.

▼ The blocks should measure 9½" x 9½" unfinished.

▼ Lay out the fabric #2 – 9½" x 9½" squares, #5 – 9½" x 9½" squares, fabric #1 – 3½" x 9½" rectangles (for sashing), and the remaining #3 – 3½" squares and nine-patch units for cornerstones as shown in the quilt assembly diagram, paying close attention to the color placement.

▼ Sew the blocks and sashing strips into rows; sew the sashing strips and cornerstones into rows.

▼ Sew the rows together to complete the quilt top.

▼ Quilt, bind, add a label, and enjoy!

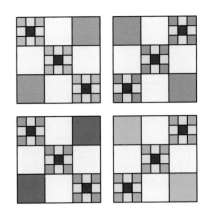

Make 1 block in each of 4 colors.

Quilt assembly

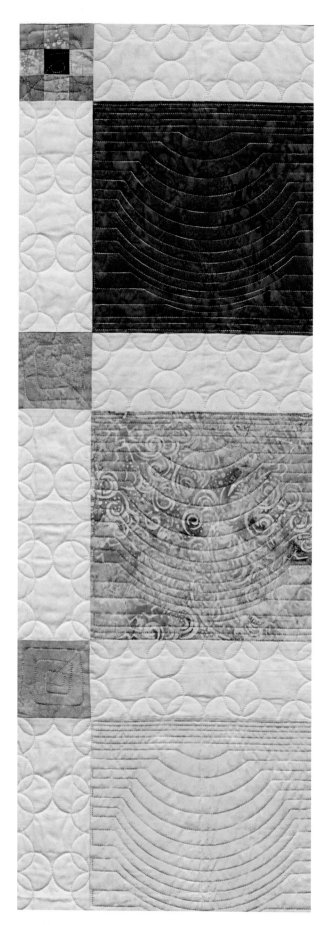

Thoughts about the Quilting from Carolyn

This quilt was a challenge for me at first because the layout and actual design feature very traditional piecing. Yet I knew the emphasis and color arrangement were modern in nature. After studying the quilt top I quickly settled on the Orb pattern by Anita Shackelford for the large blocks, but I had a hard time deciding on a modern-looking background pattern. I finally picked a simple curve pattern by Kim Diamond and created bubbles all through the background. This was the perfect combination because I love the almost 3-D effect it created! It just proves it is worth taking your time when deciding on a quilting pattern until the perfect idea presents itself. Let the fabric and design "speak" to you when deciding how to quilt a top.

I always have lots of "help" in my sewing studio when I sew. When I was piecing SATURATED COLOR PLAY, Toby wanted to play with the fabrics, too!

LEFT: SATURATED COLOR PLAY, detail. Full quilt on page 101.

SNACK MAT, 8" x 16", made by the author

Round 2 Re-do: Two-Hour SNACK MAT

Use your leftover squares to whip up a pretty, rainbow-colored snack mat in just a couple of hours. I trimmed colorful squares from several of my projects to 2½" x 2½" and pieced them in a rectangular layout. Using a leftover scrap of Fusi-Boo® Fusible blended batting by Fairfield Processing, I was able to machine quilt diagonal straight lines and finish this fun little addition to my desk in less than two hours. It's a great way to spend an afternoon so I hope you'll give it a try!

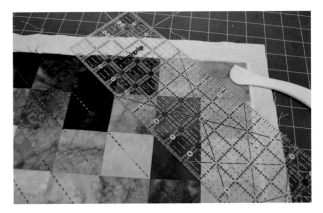

I used a Clover® Hera marker and ruler to create simple, diagonal lines to quilt my snack mat.

Variegated, rainbow-colored 30-wt. cotton thread adds the perfect touch of color and pizzazz to this little project.

Resource Guide

Contributors

It is with sincere and heartfelt appreciation I would like to thank the following companies and individuals for their support of products and services that have helped to make this book possible. The fabric, batting, tools, machines, and supplies featured or mentioned in this book are listed because they are truly the products I love and rely on to create my own quilts. I'm frequently asked about my choice of products and I'm happy to list them here so you, too, can buy and use these top quality items to enhance your own quilting experience and results. They can be purchased at your local quilt shop, sewing machine dealer, on the Internet, or by mail order. I hope you'll give them a try, and please let them know that I told you!

EZ Flying Geese Ruler (formerly Easy Star and Geese Ruler)
EZ Jelly Roll Ruler (formerly Simpli-EZ Jelly Roll Ruler)
EZ Dresden Tool / EZ Fat Cats Tool
You can order these tools directly from me at my website or:
www.kimberlyeinmo.com
www.simplicity.com

Robert Kaufman Fabrics
129 West 132nd Street
Los Angeles, CA 90061
Phone: 800-877-2066
www.robertkaufman.com

Timeless Treasures Fabrics
483 Broadway, 4th Floor
New York, NY 10013
Phone: 212-226-1400
www.ttfabrics.com

Fairfield Processing Corp.
P.O. Box 1157
Danbury, CT 06813-1157
Phone: 800-980-8000
www.poly-fil.com

Aurifil
184 Shuman Blvd. Suite 200
Naperville, IL 60563
Phone: 312-212-3485
info@aurifilusa.com

BERNINA of America
BERNINA 820 QE and accessories
3702 Prairie Lake Court
Aurora, Illinois 60504
630-978-2500 ext. 640
www.bernina.com

Koala Cabinets / Tacony Corporation
1760 Gilsinn Lane
Fenton, MO 63026
Phone: 636-349-3000
www.sewingandcraftclub.com

American Quilter's Society
P.O. Box 3290
Paducah, KY 42002-3290
Phone: 270-898-7903
www.americanquilter.com

Electric Quilt Company
419 Gould Street, Suite 2
Bowling Green, OH 43402-3047
Phone: 419-352-1134
www.electricquilt.com

Rowenta USA
2199 Eden Road
Millville, NJ 08332
Phone: 800-ROWENTA
www.rowentausa.com

Karen Kay Buckley Scissors
www.karenkaybuckley.com
Phone: 717-258-4111

Prym Consumer USA, Inc.
950 Brisack Rd.
Spartanburg, SC 29303
Phone: 864-576-5050
www.dritz.com/brands/
omnigrid/index.php

The Simplicity Creative Group
6050 Dana Way
Antioch TN 37013
Phone: 800-545-5740
www.ezquilt.com

Olfa-North America Division
9525 West Bryn Mawr Avenue,
Suite 300
Rosemont, IL 60018
Phone: 800-962-6532
www.olfa.com

Clover Needlecraft Inc.
1441 S. Carlos Avenue
Ontario, CA 91761
Phone: 800-233-1703
www.clover-usa.com

Schmetz
3800 West 42nd Street
Chicago, IL 60632
www.schmetzneedles.com

The Strip Stick
Babb Enterprises
Phone: 409-656-3013
www.thestripstick.com

Jillily Studio Needle Arts
15083 Bugle Ridge Dr.
Herriman, Utah 84096
Phone: 801-234-9884
www.jillilystudio.com

Longarm Machine Quilting Sources

Birgit Schüller/Creative BiTS
Schachtstrasse5
66292 Riegelsberg
Germany
Email: birgit.schueller@
creativebits.biz
Web: www.creativebits.biz

Carolyn Archer/Ohio Star Quilting
2895 Wilmington Road
Lebanon, OH 45036
Phone: 513-933-9008
Email: carcher3@roadrunner.com

Christine Lacroix/Quilt Patch Deco Quilting
Email: Christine@quiltpatchdeco.com
Web: www.quiltpatchdeco.com

Judi Madsen/Green Fairy Quilts
Phone: 801-867-9455
Email: greenfairyquilts@yahoo.com
Web: www.greenfairyquilts.com

Shelly Pagnali/Prairie Moon Quilts
34374 Menefee Road
New Cambria, MO 63558
Phone: 660-676-0606
Email: shelly@prairiemoonquilts.com
Web: www.prairiemoonquilts.com

About the Author

Kimberly Einmo is an author, award-winning quilter, designer, international quilting instructor, and quilt judge. She has written four books published by the American Quilter's Society including *Quilt a Travel Souvenir*, *Jelly Roll Quilts & More*, *Jelly Roll Quilt Magic*, and *Precut Bonanza*, which were all bestsellers. And now, her fifth book, *Modern Quilts & More* is sure to be another bestseller!

Kimberly is host to four immensely popular online quilting courses, featured on **Craftsy.com**, and she has also appeared on television and radio programs such as *America Quilts Creatively* and *Pat Sloan's American Patchwork and Quilting Radio* show. She has written many articles and designed original patterns which have appeared in publications including *American Patchwork and Quilting*, *McCall's Quilting* and *Quick Quilts* magazines, *Best Modern Quilts*, *American Quilter*, *Quilters' Home*, *Studios*, *Japanese Patchwork Tsushin*, *Down Under Quilts*, and *Irish Quilting* magazines.

Kimberly has also developed a signature line of innovative tools including the EZ Flying Geese Ruler, EZ Jelly Roll Ruler,

KIMBERLY einmo ••••• modern QUILTS & more

EZ Hearts Cut Tool, and the EZ Pineapple Ruler, all manufactured and distributed by EZ Quilting. She has traveled the United States and the world extensively to lecture and teach, and she represented the United States at the second, fourth, and sixth Annual Prague Patchwork Meetings in 2008, 2010, and 2012. Kimberly has taught on many quilting cruises with Quilt Seminars at Sea, and she will return to the high seas for cruises to Alaska, the Caribbean, New England/Canada, Mexico, and beyond.

Kimberly is a member of the prestigious group of BERNINA Sewing Ambassadors of America, and has also represented Pfaff Sewing Machines as one of their Pfaff Sewing Stars. Most of all, Kimberly loves to meet quilters from around the world and share the joy and passion of patchwork with everyone!

Website: www.kimberlyeinmo.com
Email: Kimberly@kimberlyeinmo.com

Fun Fact from Kimberly!

Quilting is my passion, but a little-known fact about me is that I share another passion with my family—scuba diving! Kent and I became certified divers when we were both in our teens and since both our boys have recently become certified PADI divers, we have been able to participate in this fun and amazing recreational sport as a family. Now we love to plan our vacations to visit dive sites around the globe (destinations with quilt shops located nearby, of course!).

more AQS Books

This is only a small selection of the books available from the American Quilter's Society. AQS books are known worldwide for timely topics, clear writing, beautiful color photos, and accurate illustrations and patterns. The following books are available from your local bookseller, quilt shop, or public library.

#8523 . . . . . . $26.95

#8146 . . . . . . $26.95

#8761 . . . . . . $21.95

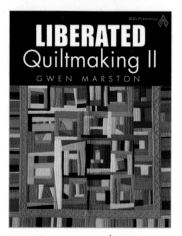

#8147 . . . . . . $28.95

#1418 . . . . . . $26.95

#8763 . . . . . . $24.95

#8664 . . . . . . $19.95

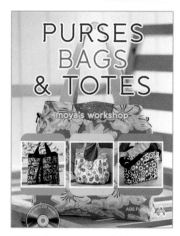

#8764 . . . . . . $22.95

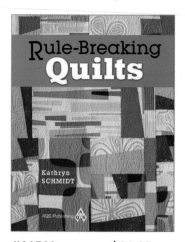

#8150° $24.95

LOOK for these books nationally.
CALL or **VISIT** our website at

1-800-626-5420
www.AmericanQuilter.com